Charles Ingersoll

A Brief View of Constitutional Powers,

showing that the Union consisted of independent states united

Charles Ingersoll

A Brief View of Constitutional Powers,
showing that the Union consisted of independent states united

ISBN/EAN: 9783337036881

Printed in Europe, USA, Canada, Australia, Japan

Cover: Foto ©Suzi / pixelio.de

More available books at **www.hansebooks.com**

A

BRIEF VIEW

OF

CONSTITUTIONAL POWERS,

SHOWING

THAT THE UNION CONSISTED

OF

INDEPENDENT STATES UNITED.

PHILADELPHIA.

1864.

Constitutional Powers.

In England, which is a constitutional government, one of the limitations of the central power, that of the monarch who commands the military forces, is the custom of making the Mutiny Act an annual one. Continuing in force but one year, Parliament, which therefore cannot be prorogued beyond that period, or either House thereof, by refusing to re-enact it, can paralyze the military organization which pervades that mighty empire, and in one instant plunge it into anarchy. And were the occasion to arise, in which either element of that government were to clearly perceive its existence aimed at by the others, can it be supposed that it would hesitate to use a power conservative of its being? If it believed the existing form of government an appropriate one, would it have the right to refrain from so proper a use of its reserved power? Would it not by refraining in fact lend its aid to destroy it? The military power of the kingdom is therefore only delegated to the crown, and for a year at a time. In the event supposed, the soldiery would side with the orders of the State to which they might happen to feel themselves allied, just as in this country, were the Federal Goverment to go out of existence, the different portions of the army would fall back to the States which furnished them. It is the consciousness of this that restrains the desires and moderates the views of each Estate, or State, as Webster defines it, in England; and insures a compromise on every question concerning which opinions are found to be opposite and conflicting. It is because of this that England is truly the government of a limited monarchy.

What would seem at first sight more natural than that the head of a government and commander of its armies, should have over them the absolute power of command? That in military organization the principle of obedience to its head should be fundamental? Where, however, this is so, there is always despotism; while in England and the old United States, where, also, independent, but not necessarily conflicting, powers co-existed, freedom and liberty resulted. Of England then it may be said, that certain powers are not delegated to the crown, but are reserved to the nobles or the people.

Had the Puritans, or Impuritans, as they have been called, happily for us never left their native shores, and had they increased there as rapidly as they have here, it might have been they would have organized themselves into a society for the abolition of the hereditary order of the peerage; the power that stands between the crown and the people, restraining both; and which, perhaps, less perfectly serves the purpose than, ultimately, it shall be found our sovereign States will with us. And it might have been we would never have heard of the attempted abolition of the hereditary order of negro slavery in America. If, by their sophistries, these social disturbers could have gained the people to return them in sufficient numbers to the House of Commons, to have a majority therein, and in turn have deluded the crown with an idea that the progress of humanity would be greater, were it to join them in assuming entire control of affairs, that is in usurping the whole Government, and that honest industry was an obsolete and exploded mode of acquiring wealth— it was a pitiful way at best, for one could only lay by something for a rainy day; whereas, by the printing press, Aladdin's wonderful lamp was thrown in the shade in the matter of princely fortunes, and palaces, and harems; if this could have been brought about, and a crusade for the abolition of the hereditary order inaugurated, of course the peers, to save the constitution of government, as well as with a view to self-preservation, would have rejected the Mutiny Bill. With their Beechers and Sumners, and Wades and Sewards, and Lincoln and his Leaguers, how old England would have rung, and how all her decent people would have sickened, with their howling cry of *military necessity* and *national life*. How some sophistic Binney would have urged her judges to rule, that as subordination was of the very essence of military organization, the power to enforce it was therefore to be educed from its institution; that, in short, in the absence of law his desire was to be adopted as law. Or to speak more accurately, in the absence of a law passed by the Three Estates, but not in the absence of all law, for in such a case, each Estate would have the legal and moral right to use its own law, its entire, its absolute power. And such would be its duty, for only by the three orders, each maintaining itself, could the constitution of government be preserved. But would her judges have proved faithless, and have aided him to tumble an old established government in ruins, and erect a new one thereon. No! They would have remembered the just fate of many a victim of the block-and-axe; and it may be that the pillory and the whipping-post would have tied the tongues and palsied the hands of the would-be demagogues and incendiaries, without whose wild ravings the usually calm and cautious judgment of a learned lawyer could hardly have been disturbed. The use of reserved power, while attended with disorder, would have saved England from a dreadful revolution and the loss of some of her elements of greatness. And it would be in such a case, if ever, that the doctrine of military necessity could be properly invoked; for it would be solely with a view to support and continue the existence of the legal establishments of a kingdom; in short, to use the simplest language, to preserve the constitution, and truly to save the national life.

The use of its reserved power by an establishment of a nation would seem to be entirely conservative. The constant declaration of an intention, in certain contingencies, to use it, would be entirely proper, and solely for the purpose of conservation. Indeed, such constant declaration ought to convince a reasonable mind that such was the only object. As to the assumption of power which has not been delegated, no doubt ought to exist. It is usurped, not for the purpose of conservation, but for the purpose of destruction and revolution. The intention is, by destroying other power, to attain undisputed domination.

Power is a subtle matter—beneficent in the hands of those who with chastened desires possess the art of government, but dangerous and, it may be, fatal, when wielded by the presumptuous ignoramus, the pretentious quack, or the artful and unscrupulous adventurer. The deadliest poison is used by the skillful physician to preserve life and restore health ; by the charlatan in such manner as to sacrifice both ; or by the evil-minded with the intention to destroy. And so with the knife. In the hand of the surgeon, the diseased part is removed and the blessing of health follows its use; or held by the innocent, it may deter or repel an assailant ; while the hand of an assassin may direct it with fatal effect. Its use, or the intention of him who uses it, in no wise alters the nature of the knife or of the poison. Neither is the nature of power in the least degree changed by the use thereof, nor by the intention of those who use it ; although the effects of its use may differ as widely as salvation and destruction.

Power is subtle because it is the domination of mind over matter. When the mind supposes itself to be fully instructed, its belief is entire, and the action as well as direction of the will would appear to be a mere consequence, to be almost involuntary. The mind may become further instructed, it may at last attain the fullness of knowledge of the subject, but its belief, however, is not less nor more entire; it is still nothing but belief; but it is changed, like that of him informed he had been pursuing a wrong road, and the direction of the will is also necessarily changed. But he may have been pursuing the right road, and if he believe one who deceives him, he then travels with equal confidence away from the place he desires to reach. The collected mind of a people is controlled or impelled by the same causes which affect that of the individual. Power such as we speak of, that of the collected will, is where legal establishments or institutions exist; and where the principles thereof are firmly fixed in the minds of the people, who therefore yield obedience to the heads of the respective organizations, and maintain them. This is organized power, and its efficiency and permanence are in exact proportion to the correctness of the principles on which it is based. Among nations, and also in the institutions which compose them, as is the direction of their will, so is the direction of their arms; to hope otherwise would be as idle as to expect the grass to bend against the wind. Consequently in a constitutional government, the declaration of an intention to destroy an institution which the minds of the people, or of a sufficient portion of them, have maintained, and yet consent to maintain, is in reality a declaration of civil war. Now a constitutional government endures just so long as the minds of the people who live under it, consent to uphold the independent organizations which compose it; and without which there cannot be constitutional government. A constitution implies the existence of two or more social elements, and its preservation and continuance depend upon their vitality; the vitality depends upon the healthfulness of the organization; and in the organization of each element there must necessarily be not only a right of resistance, but also a power of resistance. This moderates the aims of each, and good government instead of anarchy or despotism is the result; for the same social force possesses a very different character when subject to other forces, when of equal power with them, and when itself absolute. When the consent thereto ceases, a change immediately commences, and the fall or destruction of the establishment is consummated slowly or suddenly in proportion to the unity or intensity of the public will. Consent to an institution may cease, or apparently cease, but it may be revived and become as full or fuller than before, in which event, if the organization yet remain undestroyed, the establishment would be revived, and become correspondingly strong. This occurred in England, where, after the Great Rebellion, the nobility, which as an order had not made itself obnoxious, and whose organization had not been destroyed, was fully restored; while in France, where it was destroyed, it has been found impossible, although the consent revived, to re-establish it. In this country constitutional government existed because independent States existed, and the principle thereof was implanted in the minds of the people, who therefore upheld them; and just in proportion as that principle of the mind became debased, the foundation of the independence of the States was sapped, and a new and unconstitutional principle, that of absolutism of the Executive of the Federal Government, consequently assumed sway over them.

By expressing in words on parchment their agreement to create a new organization, for certain specified purposes, to which limited powers were delegated, the States by no means agreed to surrender their independent existence; on the contrary, their words and terms are clear and express as to their own perpetuity, to say nothing as to the actual fact of their continued existence. And they provided, too, that at their will they can alter their agreement, that is, alter the government which they made. They certainly never agreed that their agreement could alter itself. This, preposterous as it sounds, would have been the case, if, as is held by some, the Executive can, by being himself the sole interpreter, disregard the limitation upon him, and wield such power as he claims to have the right to decide he possesses. Of course he would decide that he held sufficient to enable him to effect any object that he conceived to be proper, which would be supreme and absolute power. If every one connected with the Federal Government were united with the Executive in such view, it would not alter the position, for every one of the States could hold an opposite view; and in such a case it would scarcely be contended that the Federal Government could rightfully defy their will. If this be not so, what was meant by the provision that in making alterations, the States should proceed according to certain forms? Why provide for alterations at all, and by a cumbrous and tedious mode, if the Executive himself can in an instant effect the change; for if he can do so, he can also disregard the alteration. If the minds of the people consent to this, if they consent that the States shall no longer remain independent, but be mere phantoms of departed powers, then the Federal Executive is absolute, and wields all power, and the constitution of government is gone, for there will remain only a people and their master, whose will is their only law.

The constitution consists in the union and agreement of independent powers, and endures only so long as those independent powers endure. By being reduced to writing, the declarations of the supreme law of the States, not of the Government of the United States, but a law governing that government, are not made more binding, but they are more readily understood, and become more widely and distinctly known. The words used are not the constitution—they indicate the intentions of the States which form it, they express the terms of agreement that have been settled by the States, but they are no more the constitution than a certificate is a marriage, and there has been many a valid marriage without a word of writing, to which the unwritten constitution of the Three Estates of England may be compared; and much writing, often, where there was no real marriage, as in the middle ages, when ceremonies were performed in the names of children who could not yet speak; and who, from early death, never attained the power implied in the terms of the pretended compact. This fallacy of taking the word for the thing, the shadow for the substance, has deluded the people of many modern nations into the belief, that, by engrossing on parchment pretentious words, and provisions and conditions, they were making constitutions. Being based upon nothing, that is, there being no pre-existing independent powers, first to agree upon, and afterward, for which continued existence is essential, to support and enforce, the conditions and provisions, these visionary productions of the dreamer last just so long as their provisions and conditions are not required to restrain the use of power. The moment this occurs by any one invoking them to protect himself against the executive, who, in a consolidated nation, necessarily directs all organized power, they fail; the only one to enforce the conditions being the individual himself. These mock constitutions, therefore involve the impossible necessity that any one who would rely upon one of their provisions, should organize a sufficient combination in his aid, for what individual is strong enough to war against a government. What plan and specification in writing of a dam across a river, would even stop for one instant the flow of the current? In quiet times when it is scarcely more than a gentle rill, parchment would almost be sufficient, but when the waters rise, and the torrent roars, and the howling tempest distracts the mind, what foundation and what superstructure too strong! Then indeed is wanted the dam itself, not the words which convey the idea of a dam. Such imaginary conditions and provisions prove baseless and unsubstantial; not so, perhaps, those in the agreements of the States in the Federal Union, which still have the shades of those once independent States, with, however, perfect organizations yet existing, and only awaiting returning consent, to uphold them. These States, by the minds of their people, even now not very unequally divided on the subject, becoming again instructed, may again be independent, and by the will of the people, resume the direction of their power. Then, and not till then, will power limit power, and the citizen be free.

As to the derivation of the power that a State possesses, we are to draw upon the whole fund of English constitutional and colonial history. A very few references, however, need be made, for it is only necessary to show that the colonies were planted by subjects of the English Crown; that they were held by that crown as separate and distinct dependencies; and that in their struggle for independence they were not merged into one organization. That this has not occurred at any time since then, may be seen in the Declaration of Independence; in the Articles of Confederation and Perpetual Union, of 1781; in the articles of the Federal Union afterward agreed upon; and in each constitution of the thirty-four existing States.

Under authority from the crown, the colonies were planted by Englishmen on territory obtained by discovery, purchase, or conquest. Grants and patents were issued by the crown to individuals or companies, who exercised the authority and rights thereby vested in them, in the establishment of these new governments. When Henry VII. in in 1502, granted a licence to Elliott and his associates to discover unknown countries, and to plant them with English, he empowered the grantees "to make laws for the new settlements." (Rymer's Fed. xiii. p. 37.) In the grant of November 1620, by James I., one object is stated to be "to extend the boundaries of his dominion." This would appear to be the prominent object of the whole system of colonization.

George Chalmers, a British loyalist, who returned to England, and there for many years held the office of Chief Clerk of the Privy Council, in his Political Annals, published in 1780, says on pp. 14, 15, "It is a circumstance in the history of the charters extremely remarkable that with a spirit somewhat unaccountable they declare 'that the emigrants and their posterity shall still be considered as English subjects.' * * * We shall discover however that the most accurate of all the charters, that of Pennsylvania, contained no such declaration; an omission which arose probably from design rather than accident. That illustrious statesman and lawyer, the Lord-Keeper Guildford, perused it with attention, and adjusted its various clauses. When William was about to renew the charter of Massachusetts, soon after the Revolution, he was advised, by the ablest lawyers in England, that such a declaration was nugatory; because the law necessarily inferred, that the colonists were Englishmen, entitled to the rights and burdened with the duties of Englishmen. If the clause before mentioned was futile, the reservation of a right of legislation with regard to the Colonies in the Supreme Magistrate was undoubtedly illegal. For whatever was the opinion or practice of James I. and his immediate successor, a King of England at no period of its annals could legislate for his people without the consent of the State." His access to the English State Papers gives great value to the authority of this writer. On page 17, he says: "It seems certain, that though such exertions of prerogative were very common in that age, a King of England could no more exercise a legislative authority over English subjects because they had removed to a distant territory of the State, than over Englishmen within the realm."

"Massachusetts, Rhode Island and Connecticut were chartered colonies, enjoying systems altogether democratical, without yielding to England the unsubstantial appearance of sovereignty. New Jersey, Pennsylvania, Maryland

and Carolina were proprietary plantations, in which the
lords of the soil having derived from the same source the
equal rights by counts-palatine enjoyed, stood in the place
of the king; who possessed within their limits neither the
means of effectually executing what the supreme legislature
had enacted, nor the undefined authority which superintend-
ence may claim. In the royal governments of Virginia,
New York and New Hampshire, the Governor, the Council,
the Delegates, formed a miniature of the King, the Lords,
and the Commons."

While the grant of power to a colony, by the crown, was
liberal, the colony was still more liberal in its exercise of
it, and in an assumption of it even beyond the grant or
charter. It was by no means intended to grant sovereign
power, yet the acts of some, perhaps of all, of the colonial
governments, encroached thereon. In 1692 the Assembly
of New York passed a "Bill of Rights." Most of the others
did the same, but they were "rejected by the king because
it was thought incongruous for the legislative power of a
province to declare on what terms it would be connected
with the nation." Major John Child, 1649, published a
pamphlet "New England's Jonas cast up in London"
Speaking of Winslow, the New England agent, he says,
"And by the way, mark, reader, his great boasting, that they
are growing into a nation, high conceit of a nation, broad
high thoughts of themselves, which make them usually term
themselves a State; call the people their subjects." During
the years 1627, 8 and 9, the Governor of Virginia, in giving
certain authority to William Cleybourne, styled him the
"the Secretary of State of this kingdom, as that most ancient dominion was then called." (Chalmers', 227.) The
governments of Massachusetts, Maryland and Virginia
erected mints and coined money, ever held, in England, to
be an exclusive prerogative of sovereignty. In May 1666
the Assembly of Maryland passed an act for the naturalization of aliens. "An Act of naturalization of one colony

—14—

cannot assuredly operate in any other, because all are independent and co-ordinate." (Ibid, 316). The disputes of
all the colonial governments with that of England, and with
the crown, as to their right to lay taxes on them, also a prerogative of sovereignty, were incessent : Spotswood wrote
to the Board of Trade, in June, 1718, " The people were
made to believe that the Parliament could not lay any tax
(for so they called the rates of postage) on them without
the consent of the General Assembly."

By the charter of June 1665, Carolina was declared independent of any other province, but subject immediately
to the Crown of England. Governor Pownal in his " Administration of the Colonies," 1765, p. 37, says, " Nor is it
more necessary to preserve the several [colonial] governments subordinate within their respective orbs, than it is
essential to the preservation of the empire to keep them
disconnected and independent of each other; they certainly
are so at present." Dr. Franklin seems to have a clear
view of the subject. He says " It is an old observation of
politicians and frequently made by historians, that small
states always best preserve their manners. Whether this
happens from the greater room there is for attention in the
legislature, or from the less room there is for ambition and
avarice, it is a strong argument among others, against an
incorporating union of the colonies in America, or even a
federal one that may tend to the future reducing them under one government." (Sparks' Franklin ii. 329).

The Congress of the Colonies, which John Adams says
" was only a diplomatic assembly" (Adams' Defence, iii.
305) declared that they "are, and of right ought to be, free
and independent states," not one consolidated state as was
desired by New Hampshire, which unanimously instructed
her delegates " to join with the other colonies in declaring
the thirteen colonies a free and independent state, provided
the regulation of their internal police be reserved to their
own provincial assembly." On the 10th of October, 1780,

the Continental Congress resolved that the unappropriated lands that may be ceded or relinquished to the United States by any particular state, "be settled and formed into distinct republican states, which shall become members of the federal union, and have the same rights of sovereignty, freedom and independence as the other states."

It would appear then that the only grants of power to either of these colonies, were made by the Crown of England. That the inhabitants thereof, if not aliens, were, and were possessed of the legal rights of, English subjects. That there was an entire assumption and exercise of sovereignty by each state in the joint declaration of independence. And that there was a full recognition, for no one questions that, of that sovereignty in the Articles of Confederation and Perpetual Union, of 1781. The derivation of sovereignty from the Crown of England is therefore clear, except as to one point, which is, that that crown denied such sovereignty until in 1783, by the Treaty of Paris, the King of England recognized the independence of the thirteen States, each by its name. By this act George III. fulfilled the prophecy, which Shakspeare, in the last scene of King Henry VIII. imputes to Cranmer respecting King James—that

> Wherever the bright sun of heaven shall shine
> His honour, and the greatness of his name,
> Shall be, *and make new nations.*

Sovereign power passed from the Crown of England to each State. A State holds and possesses its territory, but the territory is not the State. The second part of the constitution of Massachusetts says a State is, a body politic formed by a voluntary association of individuals: Article IV. of the Bill of Rights of the same State is as follows: "The people of this Commonwealth have the sole and exclusive right of governing themselves, as a *free sovereign* and *independent* State; and do, and forever hereafter shall, exercise and enjoy every power, jurisdiction, and right, which is not, or may not, hereafter, be by them *expressly delegated* to the *United States* of America, *in Congress assembled.*"

When the "Articles of Confederation and Perpetual Union," of 1781, proved inadequate, a convention of the States was called " to amend them," and met in May 1787. It was attempted to do much more than amend them. The convention framed a new plan of government containing so little of the federal principle that it met with an opposition, that at last essentially modified it. Yet the plan proposed was claimed by all its advocates to be truly federal, and as such they urged it with arguments of transcendent ability upon the States for their adoption. That there were entertained opposing views, almost impossible of adjustment, and that differences existed, radical in their nature, which were to be compromised, is proved by the well-weighed words of Washington, who, on the 31st of March 1787, wrote, " I am fully of opinion that those who lean to a monarchical government, have either not consulted the public mind, or that they live in a region which is much more productive of monarchical ideas, than is the case in the southern States." (Sparks' Wash. ix, 247.) April 25th, 1788, he wrote, "That the proposed constitution will admit of amendments is acknowledged by its warmest advocates. * * * Upon the whole, I doubt whether the opposition to the constitution will not ultimately be productive of more good than evil." (Ibid. ix, 351-2.) To speak with entire accuracy, it may be said that with all the efforts made, the States could not be brought to accede to the proposed plan. Literally speaking, they did, but practically they did not, for when at length a sufficient number of them had done so, it was with recommendations of amendments by seven of them. The States at once removed the objectionable features of the plan, by ordaining the famous articles known as the "ten amendments," so that it was in truth the amended plan of government which became effective; for the congress of the new government commenced its existence on the 4th of March 1789, and on the same day passed the amendments. At this time all the States had ratified except Rhode Island and North Carolina. It was not until April 30th, nearly two months subsequently, that Washington was inaugurated President. New Jersey, on the 20th of November, 1789, was the first, and Virginia on the 15th of December 1791, was the last State, to ratify the amendments. These ten amendments were enacted simultaneously with the establishment of the new government, and prevented, and will ever continue to prevent, it from becoming one consolidated empire, which in time would otherwise undoubtedly have been its fate. It is important to bear in mind that the well known volume, called "The Federalist," contains the arguments in favor of the proposed plan, while the arguments and articles against it, and which secured the amended plan, are not known. This ignorance has no doubt much obscured the mind of the country as to its constitutional history. Not foreseeing the violation of the fundamental rights of the people, and to account for the absence in the proposed plan of government, of a Recognition of Rights, Washington, on the 28th of April 1788, wrote to the Marquis de La Fayette, " for example, there was not a member of the convention, I believe, who had the least objection to what is contended for by the advocates for a *Bill* of *Rights*, and *Trial* by *Jury*. The first, a Bill of Rights, where the people evidently *retained* everything, which they did not in *express terms give up*, was considered nugatory." (Ibid. ix, 357.) The words, " give up," correctly express the fact as it existed at the time the letter was written, for Article 1, Section 1, of the constitution, by the use of the word " granted," conveyed power absolutely, as a gift; but subsequently, by the action of the States and the Federal Government, this absolute gift was entirely reclaimed; for by the amendments, the powers of the Federal Government are not granted or given, but are merely " delegated." By the use of the word *delegated*, in Article X, of the amendments, each State retains the right of judgment as to the use of the power it had delegated. No mis-appre-

3

hension as to this is possible, for, aside from the well-known meaning of the word, John Adams had just quoted from Milton's "Ready and Easy way to Establish a Free Commonwealth," "In this grand council must the sovereignty, not transferred, but *delegated only*, and, as it were, deposited, reside." (Adams' Defence, 2d ed. 1794, i, 366.) To illustrate how clear it is that each State is the judge of the use of the power it has delegated, suppose New York were by all the other States reduced to one senator, in violation of the provision for the equal senatorial representation. Would not New York be the judge of that invasion of her right? Would the very States which invaded it be the judges thereof, and she, the State aggrieved, be the only one with no right of judgment, and with no right to use her power to redress the wrong?

Some observations on the nature of the Government that was created, and a review of certain opinions entertained of it, may not be inappropriate before a further consideration of the question, whether it was a mixed one, of divided powers, that is, limited; or whether it was, what it it is now held by some to be, a government of unlimited powers, an absolute despotism. John Adams was so opposed to the principle of arbitary power that he wrote, " It may sound oddly to say that the majority is a faction; but it is, nevertheless, literally just. If the majority are partial in their own favor, if they refuse or deny a perfect equality to every member of the minority, they are a faction." (Ibid. iii, 287.) His work was entitled, "a Defence of the Constitutions of Governments of the United States of America against the attack of M. Turgot in his letter to Dr. Price." Mr. Turgot had complained that in America, " instead of collecting all authority into one centre, that of the nation, they have established different bodies, a body of Representatives, a Council, and a Governor." It was Mr. Adams' successful effort to answer the complaint. He claims to prove that " without three orders, and an ef-

fectual balance between them, in every American constitution, it must be destined to frequent unavoidable revolutions."
(i, ix.) "There would be an end of everything were the
same man, or the same body to exercise the three powers,
that of enacting laws, that of executing public resolutions,
and that of judging the crimes or differences of individuals." (i, 154.) "Now it is impossible to balance two assemblies; without introducing a third power, one or the
other will be most powerful, and whichever it is, it will continually scramble till it gets the whole." (i, 212.) As the governor and members of both houses of the legislature, and
the judges, too, are now chosen by the same electors, it is a
consequence, that a political party, which may secure them
all, has them for *its* representatives, and occupies precisely
the position of the successful one of the two assemblies
which Mr. Adams supposes. His balance therefore proves
defective, as must ever be the result where the fallacious
system of a simple arithmetic plan of representation is attempted; and the country is now in the condition into
which he foresaw it would be plunged without a balanced
government.

"Three branches of power have an unalterable foundation
in nature; they exist in every society, natural and artificial;
and if all of them are not acknowledged in any constitution
of government, it will be found to be imperfect, unstable
and soon enslaved." (i, 362.) With the observation that
"the congress of the confederation was not a legislative
nor representative assembly, but only a diplomatic assembly," (i, 363,) he goes on to say that "Dr. Price and the
Abbe de Mably are zealous for additional powers to Congress. Full power in all foreign affairs, and over foreign
commerce, and perhaps some authority over the commerce
of the States with one another, may be necessary; and it is
hard to say, that more authority in other things is not wanted; yet the subject is of such extreme delicacy and difficulty,
that the people are much to be applauded for their caution.'

The object of his labor is, "to collect together the ancient and modern leagues, the Amphyctionic, the Olynthian, the Argive, the Arcadian, and the Achæan confederacies among the Greeks—the General Diet of the Swiss Cantons, and the States-General of the United Netherlands, the Union of the Hanse-Towns, which have been found to answer the purpose both of government and liberty, and consider what further *federal* powers are wanted." (Ibid. i, 364.)

Mr. Adams, whose work was first issued in 1787, prior to the meeting of the Federal Convention, and with the purpose to instruct the members thereof, was entirely correct in his judgment that without a balance in the government of a state, its history must necessarily present a continued scene of anarchy and end in slavery. But a fallacy lay in his supposition that *three paper orders*, here an ideal scheme, a form merely, borrowed from the reality in England, would prove a balance. They cannot, for they repose on nothing. With a view to such an end, and to protect minorities, for majorities, to some extent, can protect themselves, it was proposed in Massachusetts, by her convention of 1853, to wisely provide for an unequal apportionment of representatives, which in some degree results in a temporary balance of power. "The population of Fall river is 11.700, and is entitled to *three* representatives. There are twenty-three towns in other parts of the state, with a population of 11,308, which are entitled to *twenty-three* representatives, etc., etc." (Discussions on the proposed Constitution, 214). In the state of Delaware, each county, whatever its population, has an equal representation, both in the senate and in the house; and it will be found, that this is a near approach to a true constitution, going far to preserve her good government.

The colonists who came to this country were generally of the democratical class. They came with the ideas, the mind, of England, fully recognizing, as it did, the three established orders in that kingdom; but they did not bring the three orders with them. They came as a democracy, or commons, yet with minds so disciplined that until recently they have considered that a positive limitation of their power did in reality exist. To speak only of the Northern States in this connection, party division and doctrine aided to support this opinion, which, however, gradually yielded to the subtle teachings of the New Englander, who, unable to gain a livelihood from the sterile soil of his nativity, sought it where nature was more bountiful, and among a people who were happily content with their lot. Such a people could only be deluded into a consent to abandon their fair inheritance and their worship of the true God, by the promise of this tempter, that he would give them all the States of the Union and the glory of them, if they would fall down and worship him. While the mind in the Northern States had gradually reached this condition, from which, however, perhaps as to the greater part, it has, through the purifying teachings of the past four years, now recovered, that of the Southern States has, also gradually, reached one exactly the opposite. There, along with the first planting of those colonies, was founded an establishment much resembling that of caste of the empires of antiquity, or serfdom of the middle ages. This institution has so entwined itself in the social and political relations of those States, that, with accelerating intensity, its necessary consequences have dominated the minds of the people more completely than serfdom ever did in England; for even in the time of Edward I., the serfs were less numerous than these slaves now are, and they were not fixed in their position by the law of race and color. The mode of government, too, of the serf, was not so exactly adapted to his nature and his wants, as that under which the negro lives so happily and becomes so elevated, that he furnishes the novelist with that modern marvel, an "Uncle Tom."

Apart from this radical division of the whole American mind, it is important to consider the long existing and marked difference of character between the two sections of the peopleof the Northern States. It would be most un-just, however, not to recognize that there are very many honourable exceptions to this arbitrary classification. The difference is seen in the many years of disregard by New England, of the rights of other States to the return of fugi-tives from service. In this they regard their greed, but not their right, for it is impossible that any one can regard his own, who disregards anothers rights. He strikes at the principle by which they are held; he forfeits them, so to speak. The existence of rights repose only and surely upon arms; and the absence of the military spirit in New Eng-land, while it is so prevalent elsewhere in the North, proves an essential difference of character, if not of principle, and bodes ill for their retention of the rights they so recklessly peril. The preservation of personal rights has always been held, except by many among the people referred to, to be of such vital importance that they are recognized in the ar-ticles of the constitution, as above and beyond, and not de-pendent thereon. These rights were obtained only by success in arms, and they could not have been preserved except by the establishment of a government of a nature entirely limited as to its power to infringe upon them. It is in the possession of these rights that the citizen of an American State differs from the subject of any other gov-ernment, for as the subject race in a nation is the democracy, the Americans, by the prosperous issue of their war against the Crown of England, lost somewhat of the character of that class, and, in a proportional degree, assumed that of an aristocracy. It may therefore be said, that so far as the spirit prevails to maintain by arms, if necessary, their independ-ent rights as self-governing freemen, they are more exactly a democracy of aristocrats. New England, however, par-took of this changed character in a lesser degree than the other Northern States. The British forces, which scarcely made an attempt to penetrate the interior, left Boston in March, 1776, and afterward, during the long years of war, there was scarcely a hostile foot upon her soil. Her people in general had not the spirit of a warlike race. "Her soldiery, at the time I am speaking of, was contemptible in the extreme." "It was no unusual thing in the army before Boston, for a Colonel to make drummers and fifers of his sons, thereby, not only being enabled to form a very snug, economical mess, but to aid also very considerably the revenue of the family chest." (Graydon's Memoirs, 2d edition, 158, 148.) Washington wrote to Richard Henry Lee, from Cambridge, August 29th, 1775, "But it is among the most difficult tasks I ever undertook in my life, to induce these people to believe that there is or can be danger, till the bayonet is pushed at their breasts, not that it proceeds from any uncommon prowess, but rather from an unaccountable kind of stupidity. * * * * I have made a pretty good slam among such kind of officers as the Massachusetts Government abounds in, since I came to their camp, having broken one colonel and two captains for cowardly behaviour in the action on Bunker's Hill, two captains for drawing more provisions and pay than they had men in their company, and one for being absent from his post when the enemy appeared there, and burnt a house just by it. Besides these, I have at this time one colonel, one major, one captain and two subalterns under arrest for trial. In short, I spare none, and yet fear it will not all do, as these people seem to be too inattentive to every thing but their interest." (Pollard's War, Second Year, 84, 85.) On the 10th of February, 1776, he wrote, "Notwithstanding all the public virtue which is ascribed to these people, there is no nation under the sun that pays more adoration to money than they do." Although this was the impression that the Massachusetts character produced upon others, it was quite the reverse of their own opinion of themselves; for at a very early period they entered upon the dangerous career of self-deception. The Washington Federalist of February 12, 1801, says, "With the militia of Massachusetts, consisting of 70,000, (regulars let us call them) in arms; with those of New Hampshire, united almost to a man; with half the number of the citizens of the other States, ranged under the federal banner in support of the constitution"—This was in the time of the alien and sedition laws—"what could Pennsylvania do, aided by Virginia? the militia untrained and farcically performing the manual exercise with *cornstalks* instead of muskets, burdened besides with a formidable internal foe. * * * * What, may it be asked, would be the issue of the struggle?" (Sectional Controversy, 56.) A tolerably correct idea of the great difference between the two sections of the country may be formed by considering an imaginary case. Suppose a division were agreed upon, and that both armies, composed as they now are, were to take possession of the respective countries, reserving to themselves and their descendants the privilege of the suffrage. In such a case,in the Southern States, the government would be in the hands of those who own the country, comparatively few being excluded. It would be a despotism, but being, in a manner, self-imposed, its operation would be almost mild and gentle. It could not press heavily upon the hardy frames of a people not far advanced, as some have claimed, in civilization; their spirit of independence would not be broken by a rule which was their own rule. But in the Northern States, as those who own the country, would be almost unanimously excluded, the despotism of such a supposed government, would be harsh and revolting beyond any conception that could now be formed of it. The law, in each case, might be in the very same words, yet it is impossible to imagine two governments which would be in reality more radically different in nature and in character, and it may be added, in destiny.

Without considering how far so thoroughly fixed an institution as slavery might prove a balance of government, perhaps it may be correct to say that prior to the Revolution, the crown was, and since then, the Federal Union among the States has been, the actual balance of government for each State, preventing "frequent unavoidable revolutions." This is so well understood, that it may be confidentially asserted, that the principle of federation, which is a desire for, and consent of, union, is adhered to by every one, without a single exception, who adheres to the principle of the independence of each State. They may differ as to the arrangement of the details, as they have a right to do, but they do not differ as to the principle, of union. Those who do not uphold the principle of the independence of each State, can by no possibility desire a union or federation of the States. Many are indifferent, or ignorant, or visionary, or weak worshipers of the unscrupulous usurpers of power; their adoration ever rising in the exact inversed degree, to which the tyrant in his acts of monstrous brutality, may sink. But the active among them are the monarchists of whom Washington spoke. They prate of a monarchy, a limited monarchy, as they vainly imagine, and to a very much greater extent than is generally suspected. If it were possible for a monarchy to establish itself in this country, what powers are to limit it? Such a government could not be other than an absolute despotism, such, in fact, as now is almost established, and which will continue until the independence of the States be restored. The only limited governments are federative in their nature. In his barony, the baron is an absolute despot, and he can be nothing else; but when confederated with others, the monarchy they create, while itself limited by them, limits their power. And so with democratic states. They exhibit little evidence of disorder, or at least, but little attention is attracted to it, when feeble and in poverty; in which condition it is that they become confederated. The government they create is limited by their power, and it, by limiting them, saves them from anarchy. Unfortunately it is ever the tendency of these created governments, successful in baronial,

4

but not always in democratic, federations, which are apt to
separate, to swallow up or destroy their creators. The
minds of the people are led to this by their love of liberty degenerating into license. Transported with joy at
the freedom attained by federation, they strive to obtain
more, and end by losing all. The desire of the misguided
monarchists and revolutionists in this country, is not for a
union of the States, but it is to destroy the States, and to
erect one single government over the territory which belongs to them. As there would be no balance in such a
government, were it possible to erect it, anarchy and event-
ual slavery would be inevitable. The design to erect it,
will prove less practicable than the long continued and
always baffled attempts to establish an inappropriate form
of government in Mexico,where the aspiring party,whatever
it was, had at least this merit, that it existed throughout the
nation. But in this country,a century of warfare,if the supply
of unfortunate conscripts, deluded negroes, entrapped foreigners and veteran bounty-jumpers, were to continue that
long, would not suffice to make the traders and sophists of
New England the dominant military power, with their head
assuming the form, and soon the name, of Emperor. The
veiled and delusive scheme,upheld as such schemes usually
are, by many men of the purest intentions, would fail ; and
their mistaken efforts, instead of resulting in "one nation"
and "one government," would render it impossible "to
secure ourselves from the fate of the divided republics of
Italy and South America."

A thorough knowledge of the career of national life from
its birth through its various transitions to old age, decrepi-
tude and death, irresistably leads the well-balanced mind
to the conviction that the form of government, if it continue to be appropriate, should, and necessarily must, vary
with, and be adapted to, the maturing national character.
M. Comte, the most zealous of anti-feudalists, renders the
thanks of posterity to the feudal system for the good it has

done in forming modern civilization at a time when it was a necessity. In treating of our long established political institutions, the fact is not to be disregarded, that the mind of this country has already undergone all the earlier transitions through the feudal system, not in this country, but at their old homes in Europe, from which, as emigrants, they brought the exact degree of civilization which had been attained at the moment of their departure. American civilization, therefore, while in its origin European, is, at the same time, that of a more advanced era of national life. Now as a people cannot recede to a system that is past, and past forever, so far as they are concerned, the hopes of some, and fears of others, of the establishment of an aristocracy here, other than in the degree already referred to, are the idlest which can be indulged. They are simply preposterous. An Aristocracy, the rule of the bravest, according to the true meaning of the word, is a race of warriors; and where all are warriors, they only are called the best. There is usually a serf or subject race under them. It is characteristic of them that they will do little else but fight and govern. Their advent is with the birth of a nation, and dependent on bravery alone, they are, except where honour is concerned, the reverse of exclusive in their intercourse. If of their own race, the individual of merit, may, by proper means, easily reach exalted rank; but they never permit, if they can prevent it, the inferior race to be elevated to their own position. As they are the soldiers of the nation, no standing army can be required; and by preserving the independence of the country, they likewise maintain their own liberties. The existing era of our national life, or rather, of that of a part of the country, is that in which an element of an exactly opposite nature aspires to domination. It is an element benificent and liberal, if properly controlled, but it is most apt to run wild. This is now the period when city wealth, money got in trade, and manufactures, and commerce, the Plutocratic element, manifests its peculiar spirit.

It was this class, no member of which could enter the superior or governing order, owing to the injustice and mistaken policy and changed character of its worn-out aristocracy, that, produced the revolution in France. Yet it did not profit thereby; for, as De Tocqueville says, "its personal sufferings were greater, and its substantial losses relatively almost as great as that of the nobles. Its trade was partially its manufactures were totally destroyed." (Memoirs and Remains, i, 236.) This class will do almost everything else but fight; they desire an absolute government, but they aspire to be the dominant class. Lacking ever characteristic of an aristocratic order, in their pretension thereto, they resemble the well-dressed imposter who attempts to pass a worthless check. They appear in the old age of national life, and wealth being their only measure of distinction, exclusiveness in their most marked characteristic. The soldiers they hire to defend the state always deprive the people of their liberty, that of the class which employs them, faring no better in this respect, than that of the agricultural class. And this cannot be otherwise; for the very fact of the existence of such an army, proves the exhaustion of those social forces which had originally created, and may have long successfully conducted, the now tottering frame of effete government. When entirely devitalized, it necessarily falls into the hands of the army, which has the advantage of being a new and vital, and therefore dominant, organization; and its head, the successful general, if that be his and its fortune, must become the master of the country. But this can only occur when the army is composed of the people of the country, not of foreigners. In the fall of the Roman Empire, one of the boasts of which had been, that none but a Roman citizen could be a Roman soldier, "under the humane pretext of gratifying the world with a flattering title, an Antoninus, in one of his edicts, called by the name of Roman citizens the tributaries of the Roman empire. * * * * Thus

perished that ancient safety-cry which made the execution-
ers fall back: *I am a Roman citizen.*" Absolutism had
now fastened itself on the empire, and " Rome was menaced
by the Goths. The people, weary of the imperial yoke,
did not defend themselves. The men of the country, still
imbued with the old Roman manners and re ligion, those
men, the only ones whose arms were still robust and souls
capable of pride, rejoiced to see among them free men and
gods resembling the ancient gods of Italy. Stilico, the
general to whom the empire entrusted its defence, appeared
at the foot of the Alps ; he called to arms, and no one arose;
he promised liberty to the slave, he lavished the treasures
of the fisc. * * It was in vain. * * The Roman name
was abolished in the west." After this Rome produced
no great soldier, or if it did, he, like " Belisarius in tears,
left the country which repudiated the name of Roman with
as much eagerness as it formerly showed in claiming it,
when that name was synonymous with independence.''
(Thierry's Hist. Essays, XIII.) In the fall of the old French
monarchy, Anacharsis Cloots, with the tag, rag and bob-
tail of Paris, a crowd of all nationalities, at his heels, calling it the embassay of the human race, invaded the National Assembly, and demanded and obtained from it, the
restoration of the rights of man to the people of the whole
world. Fortunately for France her own people yet fill her
armies, which are therefore truly national, and the despotism of which is consequently not altogether intolerable.
Not to be outdone by these masters in the school of discord,
an American President, representing, however, only that
portion of the people which has no faith in, and is unfit for,
free institutions, and relying upon a foreign element adverse
to them, in an edict, changes, or attemps to change, the nature of the negro, by calling him a soldier, and "an American citizen of African descent."

As personal property passes rapidly from hand to hand,
the simple possession of it is usually held to be conclusive

as to title. Trained in impatience for speedy and vast results, to whose success secrecy is essential, this element of city money wealth comprehends but one mode of transacting governmental business,—a head to direct, and multitudinous clerks to be directed; and it therefore always demands a highly centralized government, a secret, silent one, like that of Venice, which was composed of merchants as rulers, aided by almost an army of spies and informers. The people of the class spoken of, bred in ease and luxury, or desiring them as the greatest earthly good, will not themselves enter the army. Forgetful that a failure to pay may involve an attempt to seize the country, they resort to foreigners, and to a system of alluring bounties; and while they require their soldiers to be the mere slaves of their wills, they at the same time, but most unreasonably, require that they should be as brave as their enemies. Accustomed to affairs being conducted by correspondence, to balance sheets exhibiting their affairs, and to the results, the property gained, which they do not care personally to see, being held by them in the shape of paper, an ideal representation, they are, when enlisted in an adventure of which they have had no experience, but which they believe promises well, the most easily deceived people in the world. Their minds are bred to a reliance upon representations made to them. If they have faith in it, the paid newspaper correspondent's statement that the greatest victory in the history of war has been achieved, satisfies them as fully as the certificate of stock in a bank soon to break, or the well executed plan of a town not yet laid out. Believing what is told them, and what they tell each other, they are as children blowing bubbles. And in this respect, the old age of national life seems like second childhood, only that in the primitive times of national youth, those who instruct are of a superior class, and are dependent too on a class still superior to themselves; and, as a consequence, they are interested not to deceive overmuch. In the later stage spoken of, those who assume the office of instructor of the public mind, while they are often mere adventurers and self-seekers, are at the same time without fixed views of life, and without a superior class to control them. Their struggle is to live from hand to mouth. They blush not at their practices of deception, the consequences of which do not follow them into the new and shifting scenes on which they are ever vanishing and re-appearing.

No well grounded objection could be urged against the system of government referred to, were it appropriate. But it is not. It is appropriate to much of New England, and to a part of the population of New York, but it is, and will probably long continue to be, most inappropriate to all other parts of the country, upon which it is attempted to be forced by a minority positively contemptible in the point of numbers. It is therefore an impossibility in its nature, and is destined to result in an ignominious failure. The power of Venice grew with the growth of her commerce, which in time becoming that of the world, enabled her to hire all the free-lancers of christendom : and as by degrees she lost her commerce, so did her power wane. Much resembling that of Venice, in degree, as well as in nature and in character, is the military power wielded by the dominant party of the North ; and it is. or rather was, based upon a similar foundation. But the commerce which could be its only support, is already almost lost ; not laid by in a napkin without increase, which was an offence,—but in four short years fallen from a tonnage of more than five millions, to but little more than one and a half millions. Truly has the merchant stripped himself for the fight ; but he purchases the southern negro to act as his proxy.

To leave the Southern States out of the question, the futile attempt to erect such a government would involve a war in which the aspiring element must, from any point of view, be doomed to utter destruction. In the first place, it would in time have opposed to it, the whole agricultural population, who, not accustomed to speedy or frequent transfers of property, which with them is mostly real, so carefully scrutinize titles that no consideration will induce a venture where a flaw is suspected. They could not readily be brought to look upon a government suddenly changed in its very nature, from one of consent to one of force, as altogether legally established. They would detect the flaw in the title. Nor are they accustomed to look upon the mercenary soldier as a good conveyancer,—except to h m-self. In the second place, the whole of the labouring classes, who would not willing permit their cherished interests to be destroyed, could not consent to it. It was its great material benefit to those two classes, that secured the success of the French Revolution. In the third place, no such attempt could have the remotest chance of ultimate success, so long as universal suffrage prevailed, for the right of suffrage and its practice, is the institution that is most deeply fixed in the mind of the people. It is the very principle of life pervading every fibre of government; and cannot be touched without peril. It or the aggressor must die. Its violation in the border states has made the people there, the eternal enemies of the wrong doer; and had the possibility been conceived that this sanctuary of freemen was to be invaded, no troops directed by the administration, could have penetrated far into, or long remained in Kentucky or Missouri. Had they understood it, their armed defence of rights would not have proved so tardy. Nor until the results, in some degree, enlightened them, did Northern people any better comprehend what was intended; much less perceive that, as it was their own organization which was violating the principle on which itself was founded, the intention portended more danger to themselves than to the not altogether helpless people of States whose alliance had been so courted by the new and powerful Southern government. Correct knowledge has come too late for elections in the Northern States to have any practical influence on the war, with its termination, however, they will, in a certain sense, cease to be a mere form. In the fourth place, by this very suffrage, and instigated by the leaders of the party in power, by city and borough, and county and state bounties, and funds of fabulous proportions for every conceivable object, among them incessant celebrations, at which are adopted the invariable resolutions that every one but themselves shall go into the army, there have already been incurred debts of such almost inconceivable magnitude, that the devastation to the country would have been less, had hostile armies swept through every State. At this moment the wealth of the North is more completely sacked than that of the South. The process is yet going on, and with ever increasing celerity, and now, cannot be stayed by those who still direct the rising whirlwind that will finally sweep themselves, deluded mortals, to destruction. .

This magic sacking of a nation's wealth, presents a spectacle of bloated ruin, like that of some mad spendthrift heir, who, by loans, contrives to dissipate in one protracted revel the fruits of long ancestral labour. How the gathering parasites applaud to the very echo his every act of folly. How willingly, if they only could, would they die for love of him. Keen as vultures, while he is blind as a bat, they fill their pockets as they chant his praise. In his straits they vow that none is richer than he, for well they know that much of what he can borrow becomes their spoil. How they scoff and sneer at the old-fashioned fools who in grief and sorrow, shake their heads at the wild doings of a youth they were disposed to love, yet of whom, in truth they had some doubts and fears. How they warn him against, and vent their curses at, such half-hearted, disaffected fellows who stand apart, and speak with ifs and buts, suggesting doubts of legal title, that the estates are entailed, not in fee: or else, speak not at all. It is a brave sight, but it has its end Inexorable time brings judgment, and a change of scene. Now, none so helpless as he, the whilom master. Fire and flood could not have done this work of paper. And how the vampire scoundrels swear they were his victims merely. Sure, never again will they trust mortal man, if one so fair could so deceive. Obedient to a time-honoured custom, they, and all the world beside, turn their backs upon him,—for nothing more is to be expected. His only friends, now, and ready as ever with wholesome counsels, are the old-times people, his father's friends.

It is a striking fact, that the class most deeply interested *against* their scheme comprises those who are engaged in it. Yet they will not be warned. There is another class which has aided them. They are the ranting and raving philosophers of the Greely and Beecher and Wendell Phillips' school, together with the apostate ministers who have abandoned the salvation of souls for the destruction of bodies ; men whose garments are red with blood, and who by making unto themselves an anti-slavery god, have just as completely dethroned the true and living One, as did their brother revolutionists in France, when, under Danton, they worshipped that foul thing they styled the goddess of reason. Could the money-getters, whose worship is of the golden calf, by any possibility, be successful in their scheme, the first act of the master or monarch they would establish, would be, as is always done in such cases, by exile and imprisonment, to rid the land, not of honourable men who hold reasonable and cherished opinions, and are content that others should do the same, and who in the fullness of time consent to, though they may regret, the necessity of a sterner yet appropriate government; not of these, but of the pests who will always disturb and never be quiet.

The idea of a union of independent governments, even when not confederated, for only equals can so associate, and the possible advantages resulting therefrom, was not novel to the minds of those who framed the system under which the American people have lived so happily. Prior to their independence, it was claimed that each Colony was an independent State, but held of the crown, just as the kingdom of Hanover was independent, yet held, in the male line however, of the Crown of England. "The sovereign, or rather the first magistrate of the monarchial republic, Neuchatel, is the King of Prussia, whose authority is limited by the great privileges of the country. The liberties of the people, though the most absolute monarch in Germany is first magistrate, are better secured than even in the most democratical Cantons of Switzerland. Personal liberty is tenderly and securely protected, as it is in England or America, where the same laws in substance or spirit prevail. No citizen can be tried out of the country, or otherwise than by the judges. All the citizens have a right to enter into the service of any foreign State, even though at war with Prussia." (Adams' Def. ii. 446, 50.)

No vague idea of the principle that " government derives its just power from the consent of the governed," could have been entertained by students of the feudal law. " There is no lord or monarch upon earth (says Philip de Comines, himself bred in courts, born 1445), who can raise a farthing upon his subjects, beyond his own dominions, without their free concession, except through tyranny and violence." (Hallam's Middle Ages, 9th ed. i. 180) " It was a fundamental principle, that every feudal tenant was so far sovereign within the limits of his fief, that he could not be bound by any law without his consent. 'The king, says St. Louis in his Establishments, cannot make proclamation, that is declare any new law, in the territory of a baron, without his consent, nor can the baron do so in that of a vavassor.'" (Ibid, i. 165.) " It is a question agitated among feudal lawyers, whether a vassal is bound to follow the standard of his lord against his own kindred. It was one more important, whether he must do so against the king.

In the works of those who wrote when the feudal system was declining, or who were anxious to maintain the royal authority, this is commonly decided in the negative. Littleton gives a form of homage, with a reservation of the allegiance due to the sovereign ; and the same prevailed in Normandy and some other countries * * * * But it was not so during the height of the feudal system in France * * * * Even so late as the age of St. Louis, born 1215, it is laid down in his Establishments, that if justice is refused by the king to one of his vassals, he might summon his own tenants, under penalty of forfeiting their fiefs, to assist him in obtaining redress by arms. The Count of Britany, Pierre de Dreux, had practically asserted this feudal right during the minority of St. Louis. In a public instrument he announced to the world, that having met with repeated injuries from the regent, and denial of justice, he had let the king know, that he no longer considered himself as his vassal, but renounced his homage and defied him." "It was always necessary for a vassal to renounce his homage before he made war on his lord, if he would avoid the shame and penalty of feudal treason. After a reconciliation, the homage was renewed. And in this no distinction was made between the king and another superior." (Du Cange. i. 196, Mat. Paris, 126, Hallam, i. 118.) The Nobles of Aragon, "were entitled, like the nobles of the sister kingdom, to defy, and publicly renounce their allegiance to their sovereign, with the whimsical privilege, in addition, of commending their families and estates to his protection, which he was obliged to accord, until they were again reconciled." [Prescott's Ferd. & Isab. i. lxxxix, xc. The application of the term, *whimsical*, to so important a law of the Aragonese feudal federation, betrays a departure from the sound philosophy which usually characterized Mr. Prescott's mind. Any law or custom differing from those to whose control we have long been subject, must of course seem more or less unnecessary, and, inasmuch, as we are not habituated to its operation, it must, to the extent that habit is a second nature, also seem unnatural, A law entirely appropriate to a very different era of national life, is, without investigation, altogether incomprehensible to us. How little, in this country, can we appreciate the value of the dual principle in government. We are aware that it appears in the spiritual and temporal Emperors in the constitution of Japan; in the Monarchy and Premiership of England; in the Sultan and Grand Vizier of Turkey, and that in the early French Monarchy, it existed in the Crown and Mayor of the Palace. It is a principle very much derided, and seems truly whimsical to those who scout at the idea of a monarch without power or authority, as it is the fashion to assert, when speaking of the English Crown. As to this law of Aragon, its existence simply, without any other evidence, and just as infallibly as in comparative anatomy the nature and character of an organic structure can be determined from a single bone, would prove that national government to have resulted from an agreement between the barons, a union of their powers; that the head thereof, the crown, was limited; and that it was well understood that it, like other crowns, would be apt to transcend its delegated powers. It further proves that the contracting parties relied upon, what it was perfectly natural for military organizations to rely upon, their own power for self protection; and that were the use of force by the crown, attempted to be pushed to the extent of extinguishing the existence of a barony, like the project, with us, of subjugating a State, and reducing it to the condition of a territory, it would result in good faith as well as self interest enlisting all the other barons in its support. In the absence of such an organic law, if the crown could have commanded force to a sufficient extent, it could have been used for the confiscation of all property and the entire subjugation and enslavement of the people. Everything would be at the mercy of a conqueror who recognized no limit to his power, except his desire. So far then from being whimsi-

cal, this wise law was founded on reason and justice, by men
of forecast; and was of a nature to be most beneficial in
moderating the aims and views of existing forces, thus
preserving the principle of constitutional government. It
was in truth a law of civilized warfare; and a protection
to all, to the strong as well as the weak, for the dominant
party of to day, might on the morrow, be found struggling
for life. How clearly then it seems to be a law dictated by
enlightened self-interest, and more important, perhaps, to .
the party apparently successful, than to that which is for the
moment, considered unsuccessful. For, suppose, in a federation, the numerically stronger parties in a contest for
domination, were to announce that they intended to recognize no limit to their use of power, as conquerers. So un-
blushing a proclamation would but nerve the less numerous
people to an effort of the homeric age; and such an effort
always rises to a pitch of valour and endurance that is ever
crowned with success. This might place at the mercy of
the scorned, the vanquished boasters, stripped of power,
with none to deny that their fate was but the fate they designed for others.

In the feudal system the barons were each independent,
because each established and maintained himself by his own
organized power. They confederated together and generally elected one of themselves as monarch, delegating to
him certain powers, but reserving to themselves all others.
Thus arose the limited monarchies of Europe, not one of
which, however, has continued limited after the loss of independence on the part of the separate powers which created it.
The loss of their independence involved also the abolition of
their entire legal system, which, as no limitation of the
central power then remained, resulted in the crown necessarily becoming absolute, and devising or adopting a legal
system of a different and altogether opposite nature. These
feudal federations were often exceedingly defective, and at
best, it has been only some happy accident that has pre-

served sufficient of the federative principle to secure a long continuance of free government. A good example of the system is afforded in the history of the constitutional kingdom of Aragon, where the twelve great nobles, who created the monarchy, installed the incumbent of the throne with the celebrated condition,—" We who are as much as you, and are worth more than you, we chose you for our lord, on condition that you will respect our laws; if not, not." The distinguishing excellence of the " General Privilege," reluctantly conceded by Peter the Great to the Cortes at Saragossa, in 1283, consists, like that of Magna Charta, in the wise and equitable protection which it afforded to all classes of the community. [Prescott's Ferd. & Isab. i. c.] When this crown became united with that of Castile, and had made the conquest of Granada. and then of America, by the re-establishment of the Hermandad, which undoubtedly, as to its illegal and incendiary features, has here been reproduced in Loyal Leagues, its power overbalanced that of the nobles, and consequently became despotic over, not them alone, but over the people also, and free government ceased in Spain; not to be restored as Prescott, perhaps vainly, supposes. For the maxims and elevated thoughts, now, existing, which he miscalls "the dormant seeds of liberty, waiting only the good time to germinate;" [Ibid, iii, 447] are not seeds, but the fruit itself. Or considering the free institutions of Aragon as a once entire and classic structure, they are merely beautiful fragments; precious relics indeed, but such as may always be found among the fallen ruins of some ancient temple of liberty.

Free government survives in England, because her conquests have not been incorporated with the kingdom, and her insular position has not necessitated large armies in the island itself; and because of the limitation of the power of the crown by the Mutiny Act. Perhaps these causes combined are in reality less potent than the territorial power of the great nobility, which is preserved in its nature and organization, and consequently in its character, by the law of primogeniture. This makes them in fact independent princes, though their strictly feudal character has ceased. It may be made as an incidental observation, that were the peerage destroyed, not only would the social and political character of England soon be changed, but by the division of property, and the destruction of the forests and parks, with a view to cultivation, the climate too, perhaps, would undergo an alteration, as in other countries, and most probably from the same causes, and much of the land might become sterile, and the population decrease and her material prosperity be lost. De Tocqueville says, " Aided by Roman law and by its interpreters, the kings of the fourteenth and fifteenth centuries succeeded in founding absolute monarchy on the ruins of the free institutions of middle ages. The English alone refused to adopt it, and they alone have preserved their independence." [Memoir and Remains, i, 428.] When free institutions have been ruined, it is impossible to conceive any other government than absolutism succeeding them, and as government of this nature has long prevailed over the whole of Asia, it would not appear that Roman law, except so far as its principle is despotic, had any relation thereto. In Europe, Roman law was resorted to, because it was widely known through the surviving literature of the fallen empire. Had there been no Roman Empire, it is not easy to see that absolutism would consequently have been of less certain, though undoubtedly it might have been of less easy, establishment. In speaking of England he appears to reverse the order of cause and effect, for the real obstacle was the continued existence of free institutions, with which absolutism is utterly incompatible; and it would therefore be more accurate to say, that it was because the English refused to abandon their own laws, thus preventing the crown becoming their despotic master, that they thereby avoided the necessity of a resort to despotic or Roman law.

Mr. John Stuart Mill considers that as in France, "a large
part of the people have been engaged in military service,
many of whom have held at least the rank of non-commis-
sioned officers, there are in every popular insurrection, several persons competent to take the lead, and improvise
some tolerable plan of action." (On Liberty, 2d ed. 201.)
It does not appear to have occurred to him that his "tolerable plan" could only result in substituting a few new officers in the places of a few old ones, without at all affecting
the vitality of the dominating military organization, and
that consequently the principle of the government would
not be in the least degree disturbed. He continues;
"What the French are in military affairs, the Americans
are in every kind of civil business. * * * * And a
people capable of this is certain to be free; it will never let
itself be enslaved by any man or body of men because these
are able to seize and pull the reins of the central administration." (Ibid. 201-2.) Fortunately for the author's rep-
utation, his book was printed in 1859. Liberty is not the
fruit of the happy conceits and telling paragraphs of ear-
nest writers. Their thoughts are often drawn, unconsciously,
from what has formerly existed, without adverting to, or
comprehending, the deeply hidden principle involved; their
delusory promises of what the future is to bring forth, are
apt to be based only on their visionary hopes, and not upon
a correct understanding of the law of cause and effect.
Ceaseless in their action and re-action, but ever varying in the
degree of intensity, opinions modify or destroy institutions;
and institutions, modify or destroy opinions. Each have
their turn. It is not exactly in either of these forms of destruction, that liberty exists—there is, necessarily, too much
of despotism for that. In their infancy institutions dominate absolutely, else they cannot reach maturity. In their
decay, adverse opinions assume despotic sway, and thus secure their fall. Rather then would liberty seem to be a
living reality through the era of the maturity of institutions;
6

and happy the nation in which that career of glory is long
protracted. The birth of liberty may thus occur. The principle of federation necessarily involves consent; consequently
it is based upon the equality of rights among the confeder-
ates; and as each is independent, he or, if a state, it na-
turally upholds any one whose views and opinions coincide
with his or its own. Hence arises difference of opinion in
the nation, and each opinion receives sufficient support
to make it respectable. Although altogether adverse to the
hopeful but fallacious view of Mr. Mill, this is real liberty,
securely planted on an enduring foundation, with the promise of a fair development; and it would appear to be not
only a direct result of the principle of federation, but to be
impossible without it; for unless there exist the organization of an independent state or baron, on which to rely for
support, each individual, in each assertion of his right,
must, for himself, which of course is a simple impossibility,
organize a combination for the purpose. Liberty, however,
cannot outlast its foundation. Hence it is, that in a land
where the vitality of its institutions or establishments has
become exhausted; where the confederate powers, be they
states, or be they barons, have lost their independence and
ceased their existence; where nothing remains but a central government and a people, that government is absolute,
and the tendency in the people is to become uniform in character and manners; and then there is, or soon will be, nothing left, and nothing even to hope for, but a sort of
Asiatic despotism.

The principle of consent among the independent powers,
and its consequence, a compromise of difference, does not
seem to have been entirely appreciated by De Tocqueville,
who, in his admirable work on this country, says "The
first difficulty which presents itself arises from the complex
nature of the Constitution of the United States, which consists of two distinct social structures, connected, and, as it
were, encased one within the other: two governments com-

pletely separate and almost independent." (Democracy in Am. Cambridge ed. 1862, i. 173) "Evidently this is no longer a Federal Government, but an incomplete National Government, which is neither exactly national, nor exactly federal." (Ibid. i. 201.) And again he says, "The most prominent evil of all federal systems is the complicated nature of the means they employ. Two sovereignties are necessarily in presence of each other." (Ibid, i 210) The principle of the system is accurately described; but the *difficulties* and *evils* he complains of, and would remove, are exactly what are required to restrain those who temporarily wield power, no matter what their intelligence or their purpose, for the consequences of violent changes are never foreseen by their enthusiastic authors; nor can they be avoided by their helpless victims. And while they serve this important end, they afford at the same time what no one more than Mr. Mills, pp. 114, 116, recognizes as an absolute necessity for liberty and freedom, varied fields for rival developments. So far then from removing such *difficulties* and *evils*, the wise statesman would thoroughly and rigidly maintain them, with the view to lead irresistably the minds of all, to perceive no other mode of settling any question except by compromise. Does not a contest for domination between two such independent powers, with separate orbits, quite resemble a quarrel of the priest and physician over a patient, for whom nature would yet do much if man would be content to do less. These necessary ministers to our welfare greatly depend for their success upon their sway over the mind; but who would tolerate for one instant a contest between the tailor and the shoemaker, as to the absolute supremacy of either in the matter of the whole apparel? Were it the latter who aspired to domination, would not any one unconsciously plagiarise, by exclaiming "Cobbler stick to thy last?"

Mr. De Tocqueville says, " In England, the constitution may change continually; or rather it does not in reality exist." (Dem. i. 126) And that the, (his twelfth edition, Paris, 1848, contains it also) "inmutability of the constitution of France is a necessary consequence of the laws." (Ibid, ii, 429) In view of the events of the five years immediately following the revolutionary efforts of 1848, may it not be said that, even if the Constitution of England do continually change, and do not in reality exist, that nevertheless the infatuated people there believe it does exist, and with a fair promise of continuance; while that of France, *immutable* though it be, restrains neither President nor Emperor. This writer's error appears to be fundamental, but it must be remembered that he " writes under the impression of a kind of religious terror produced in his mind by the view of that irresistable revolution which has advanced for centuries in spite of every obstacle, and which is still advancing in the midst of the ruins it has caused." (Ibid, i. 6.) It is possible to understand that the curse of God, imposing slavery with all its heathen horrors, for countless centuries upon the unhappy people of mysterious Africa, could strike religious terror in the mind. It is too much to say that a calm survey of the gradual fall of European feudal institutions, protracted as it was, through some hundreds of years, could do so. It could not have been to this, but, probably, it was to the tales of terror, heard amid the scenes of nameless crimes, enacted in their wild anarchy of a few short years, by a maddened people, that the otherwise justly balanced mind and gentle spirit of the accomplished Frenchman succumbed. He says "The form of government which is usually termed *mixed* has always appeared to me a mere chimera. Accurately speaking, there is no such thing as a *mixed government*, in the sense usually given to that word, because, in all communities, some one principle of action may be discovered which preponderates over the others. * * * * I am therefore of opinion, that social power superior to all others must always be placed somewhere." (Ibid, i. 331.)

Is it not now clear that, if social power superior to all others, in the sense Mr. De Tocqueville gives, be placed somewhere, it will soon be everywhere; that it will inevitably destroy the others? That when by the aid of the democratic, it has succeeded in destroying the aristocratic, principle, it will instantly turn upon its blind and faithful ally, and appear in its true colour, a despotism; which, though it may be long protracted in its duration, is, as all history shows, the closing stage of a national life that must at last end? A nation, composed as it is of families and different interests, with their varied pursuits, may well be likened to a collection or confederation of trees, in each of which and in all of which, there is óne power, the principle of life. But that power is divided by immutable laws, and may correctly be termed a mixed power, or government, for the action thereof is as well on the roots which grow downward, and are not seen, as on the limbs which grow upward, and whose increase is so slow that the nicest eye can scarce discern it. And the foliage and the fruit, too, though they be but the product of a year, result from the same power, or from one involved therewith; for the yield of fruit of its peculiar flavour, and of leaves after their own form, would seem to be the result of attendant laws or principles, co-existent with the principle of life. Philosophers who would construct their ideal governments, should have also the power to create the beings who are to live under them. Perhaps they have; for the subjects of such despotism become in time so abject, that it is scarcely possible to realize that we and they were made by the same creator. The maturity of national life is so full in its product of rich fruit, its varied enterprizes and its useful novelties, that it appears to excite in reformers the desire to direct all power exclusively to their production. But their views and doctrines tend to a stationary despotism, like that of China, and the insipid uniformity, which is the result, would seem to be as unnatural and unlawful as if, had one of those disturb-

ers the power to do so, he were, by destroying their peculiar laws of developement, to have all trees yield but one
fruit, of one size, one colour, and one flavour. Why this
invincible determination to reduce everything to one single
element? We breathe the atmosphere, but no one is mad
enough to attempt the use of the deadly gases into which it
may be resolved. Is the planetary system to fall in ruins,
because within it, one orb revolves around another, and all
around their centre, and the tendency of their motions be
centripital and centrifugal? Though we may not comprehend it, do we not believe in the Trinity? As the works
of God are more perfect than those of man, it should be
our aim to change by development only, not to destroy,
the institutions and their principles, that may happen to
exist in the land it is our lot to live in. It sometimes happens that the tree of little promise yields rich fruit, and with
time assumes a fairer form; but if either its roots or its
limbs be destroyed it can bear none at all, and there is no
other to speedily replace it. So far then from considering
the co-existence of separate and balanced powers in a nation
as an imperfection, a chimera, it is their presence in proper
proportion, and their free and healthy action, no one dominating and destroying, but each serving its appointed purpose, that presents the truest and fairest picture of perfec-
tion.

An instance of how the purest and most devoted theoreti-
cal opponent of absolutism may, when entrusted with
power, himself become tyrannical, is to be found in the
public career of Mr. De Tocqueville. In 1839 he prepared
the report of the Committee of the Chamber of Deputies on
the abolition of slavery in the French colonies: and in sending a copy of it to John Stuart Mill, he wrote, "I have not
tried to be eloquent. I have even carefully avoided irritating the colonists, which has not prevented their newspapers
from lavishing much abuse on me. But you know what
colonists are; they are all alike, to whatever nation they

may belong. They become raving madmen as soon as one speaks of justice to their negroes." [Memoirs, ii. 50.] Had it occurred to this most accomplished writer that his subject was not eloquence itself, it can scarcely be doubted that all his great powers would have been used to make it such. That his natural disposition led him to avoid irritating the colonists, only proves that he believed himself to be right, not that they were wrong; that he was conscious of being able to direct against them an amount of force which they were powerless to resist; and was aware his influence was great in proportion to the elevation and sincerity of his mistaken views, and his temperance in their enunciation. He ought to have known, to entitle him to speak so confidently, but he could not know, what colonists are; for he was not one himself. Stigmatizing newspaper opposition as lavish personal abuse, was denying to others all right to opinion, and claiming for himself infallibility. Colonists differ from the subjects of the parent government in being unheeded in argument and unheard in council, for they cannot join any one of the parties into which the nation is divided, and which, to strengthen itself, will uphold the interests of its adherents. They perceive that the intention of the home government. in its often visionary scheme of change, to be enforced against the consent of the colonists, portends to them, certainly revolution, and, if resisted, perhaps, civil war; but that as regard the home government or nation, the intention and its consummation, while an affair of comparatively insignificant proportions. must of course be thought conducive to its interests and advantageous to its policy. The possibility of a resistance amounting to war is altogether incomprehensible to it. It is not only on the subject of negroes that contemned colonists, in the estimation of a nation that believes itself all powerful, lose their reason With the exception of Brazil and Canada, the colonists of the whole of America, when they revolted, became raving madmen in the eyes of Spaniards and Englishmen;

yet the subject of "justice to their negroes," did not, in the remotest degree, enter into that mighty contest which made a continent the master of its destiny. When Virginia so long protested against sending Africans there, no doubt the English considered her people as disordered in their intellect.

Mr. De Tocqueville selects the Southern States of the Union and England and no other country, as the scenes of great and approaching revolution. "Slavery, he says, now confined to a single tract of the civilized earth, attacked by Christianity as unjust, and by political economy as prejudicial, and now contrasted with the democratic liberty and the intelligence of our age, cannot survive." [Dem. in Am. i. 490.) While history shows most clearly that institutions change with time, and often even fall by violence, it by no means appears that it is owing to external causes acting upon them, when confined to a single tract of the earth. It is usually the effect of internal causes; but it may be that these, as in the Southern States, and in the island empires of feudal Japan and semi-feudal England, can act with equal or even greater potency in an opposite direction ; and in a time of war such counteraction is so overwhelming, that a year will almost undo the work of a century of peace. Discarding prejudice, it is impossible to perceive any difference in principle, and there is none, in one man being an hereditary noble, and another an hereditary slave. If it be right that one man should be elevated, can it be wrong that another should be depressed? That Christianity attacks slavery as unjust, is claimed only by those who reject the sole authority for Christianity, for no political abolitionist does or can accept the entire bible. Slavery is simply an inside form of government, and an excellent one it has proved for the negro race. Like all others it may be improved in its character without disturbing its nature. Abolitionists only repeat, without at all adding to, what Montesquieu has said on the subject. His views are those

of one who, a witness of an institution in its expiring condition, in his own country, applied them, not altogether
philosophically, to the somewhat different and newly established serfdom of another race on another continent. Without adverting to its sanction by Divine Law, he attacks it
as " opposite to the law of nature." (Spirit of Laws, 2nd
ed. i. 339.) The exact meaning of this view is that were
the author of it to create a world, it would be one with an
alteration or improvement in that respect. Like all others
of his day, he was of course ignorant of the fact that slavery
always existed in Africa; and that, consequently, it is
natural; unless, indeed, we are to hold that to be unnatural
which is proved to be the invariable natural tendency in
certain races of man. It might as well be said that the
wonderfully organized slavery to which the red ant subjects
the black ant, (Swainson's volume in Lardner's Cabinet
Cyclopedia, London, 1840, pp. 594 to 648.) "is opposite to
the law of nature." Some writers on political economy,
ignoring the equally important science of history, have, in
their ill-judged aversion to stable institutions, proclaimed
that slavery was prejudicial, and to prove their assertion, they themselves alleged it was a cause of weak-
ness; but the severest test the world's history affords has
more than exposed the fallacy. Its contrast with such
democratic liberty as is permitted, and such intelligence
of our age as is exhibited, by abolitionists, while it makes
civilized man blush at their ignorance and falsehoods, and
sicken at their crimes, it, at the same time, forces him to
turn to Asia to seek their parallel.

A member of the French Assembly and one of the victims
of the coup d' etat, as an exile, De Tocqueville sends to the
London Times, 11th Dec. 1851, a graphic account of that
event. "In pursuance of Article 68 of the Constitution * *
* * Any measure by which the President of the Republic
dissolves the National Assembly, prorogues it, or places obstacles in the exercise of its powers, is a crime of high trea-

7

son * * * By this act merely the President is deprived of all authority." The soldiers having arrested the members of the Assembly, it was while they were confined, Dec. 2d, 1851, that "the National Assembly, decrees Louis Napoleon Bonaparte is deprived of all authority as President of the Republic." (Memoirs and Remains, ii. 182.) "If the judgment of the people of England can approve these military saturnalia, and if the facts I have related do not rouse its censures, I shall mourn for you and ourselves, and for the sacred cause of legal liberty throughout the world; for the public opinion of England is the grand jury of mankind in the cause of freedom, and if its verdict were to acquit the oppressor the oppressed would have no other recourse but in God." [Ibid, ii. 190, 1.] It is too much to expect that one nation should preserve the freedom of others. Indeed, it rarely happens that it can even preserve its own. The public opinion, as it is called, of England, or rather the sentiment of the few who write, for opinion is apt to find its expression in action or inaction, and not in words, appears to have had no appreciable influence on the course of affairs in France. It is not easy to perceive how it could have had, except by bringing on war, and had such been the result, the effect would necessarily have been exactly the reverse of what was designed; for nothing could so effectually consolidate power in France as would war with England. But no sight can be more mournful than this of the honest hearted and honourable minded man, whose every pulse beat for liberty and whose every breath chanted its praise, now amazed at the failure of the scheme he and others had devised for its security, and utterly cast down at seeing it expire, perhaps forever, in his own loved land. It was in the agony of such a mind that he wrote to his friend, Nassau W. Senior, 24th Feb. 1854, "While you preserve your aristocracy, you will preserve your freedom. If that goes, you are in danger of falling into the worst of tyrannies— that of a despot appointed and controlled, if controlled at

all, by a mob." [Ibid, ii. 260] He was, however, fixed
in his admiration of the organization of all national power under one head, the result of his incredulity as to mixed government, and of his desire as a reformer for the removal of all
barriers which might obstruct the accomplishment of favour-
ite schemes; and not less fixed in his belief that the conclusive arguments of a few nervous writers could prove a limit
to such national power, in the face too of repeated lessons
that the utmost of their ability is, by uncertain insurrection-
ary movement, to sometimes transfer the direction of it to
the hands of another, who, whatever his disposition, soon
learns that power so organized can only be used despotic-
ally; that is, in a manner strictly in accordance with the nature
of its organization. So thoroughly was this the trained
habit of his mind, that we find him in the following year
writing to Mr. Senior, 5th Feb. 1855; " Dangerous as it is
to speak of a foreign country, I venture to say that England
is mistaken if she thinks that she can continue separated from .
the rest of the world, and preserve all her peculiar institutions
uninfluenced by those which prevail over the whole of the
continent. In the period in which we live, and still more,
in the period which is approaching, no European nation
can long remain absolutely dissimilar to all the others. I
believe that a law existing over the whole continent, must
in time influence the laws of Great Britain, notwithstanding
the sea, and notwithstanding the habits and institutions,
which, still more than the sea, have separated you from us, ·
up to the present time." [Ibid, ii. 293.]

Sentimental writers, calling themselves economists, phi-
lanthrophists, and teachers of a religion with the latest im-
provements, have for many years been engaged in a crusade,
generally profitable to themselves, against such institutions
as proved obstacles in their intellectual raids. The key-note
they sounded was, that, while *their government* would be
cheaper than that of kings and lords, and even than that of the
old government of the United States, which especially they

derided, sneering at it as dominated by the slave power, and stigmatizing its glorious flag as "hates' polluted rag, shielding a pirate's deck;" it would at the same time, they said, enure to the profit of the people in a greatly increased production everywhere. In the summer of this year, 1864, they believed that everything was in their grasp. Richmond and Atlanta were the gates to the paradise they sought. Following John Bright, who recently proposed the division of the landed property of England, and whose proposition received the countenance of Richard Cobden, Andrew Johnson, in accepting the nomination for the Vice Presidency, bids for votes by proposing to divide the large estates of the South among the poor of the North. The followers of Mahomet, wielding however the sword instead of the pen, were not more lustful in their greed of empire than those sentimentalists, whose scheme, fortunately, cannot now be pushed much further, not that inexhaustable patience offers the least hindrance, but that, in their own language, it will not pay. Cotton famines and the surfeit of debt and depreciating paper money, and the reassertion of rights, almost destroyed by the schemers and vulgar jesters and buffoons who have been aping statesmen, must soon determine the limit of credulity. This was a consequence which De Tocqueville did not foresee, and England therefore may not encounter the fate he so confidently predicted; for if it be found that the strong arms and resolute wills of Southern men shall prove their sufficient defence, it can scarcely be, that the crusade against English institutions can soon or easily find a John Brown to commence, or an Abraham Lincoln to conduct it.

The thirteen English Colonies in America declared themselves, and ultimately were recognized as, free and independent States. Each by its own military power, and, by the Continental Army, all for each, had maintained its claim to sovereignty; and they agreed together for certain purposes, upon a federative union, with the provision that it should be perpetual; a stipulation found in the League of the New England colonies, 1643, and in most treaties of peace which have been made between nations. Soon after. ward they amended their agreements of union, and in their new articles called the Federal Constitution, they wisely omit-.ted a word found to be unmeaning, for they engaged, to use the very word of Washington, in an "experiment." In a written compact, in order that no misunderstanding should arise, they clearly defined the sole ends they had in view, and the . sole means they were willing to permit should be used to attain those ends. So far were they from entertaining any idea of surrendering the States as organized independent powers, that it may be truly said the prominent object of the Union was the more effectually to preserve them in that condition. That they attempted to do this, and wisely attempted it, is proved by the marvelous success of the central government they formed,—a success that continued uninterrupted until that principle was abandoned. Its career is conclusive that the federal organization was a healthy one, which cannot be the case in any nation, unless its constitution be in harmony with its social adjustments. That their plan was for them a correct one, cannot be questioned, for it would sound like a truism to say that a federal form of government is necessary for a federation. To undertake to conduct a federal, on the same principle as a consolidated, government, is a violation of its nature, and only tears it to pieces. It would not be more contradictory and convulsive, were the impossible absurdity attempted, to annually elect an hereditary monarch. Except in one respect the Federal Government is identical in principle, though not in character, with the feudal monarchies of Europe. The same social forces enter into its organization; the people being the democratic; the states, the aristocratic; and the central government, the monarchial force. While the citizen, as one of the people, is a democrat, he is, at the same time, if he have any respect for law and princi. ple, something more; for as each individual takes his part

in all branches of the government, it is essential that he
should have a threefold nature. It is his duty to maintain
his personal rights, in the preservation of which all are alike
interested,—as a member of a State, he partakes of the nature
of what might be termed its baronial independence, which,
undoubtedly, he has no right to consent shall be impaired,—
and certainly it would be wrong in him to uphold the central government, in the usurpation of power from political
bodies to which he does not belong; but with which, as a
member of a State, he is in a compact well defined in its
provisions against such assumption. It is objected that this
is a complicated system of government, but it is quite impossible to perceive that any greater intellectual effort is
necessary to understand it, than is required of most of us in
the ordinary affairs of life; scarcely more than to prevent
us confounding the offices of the priest, the lawyer and the
physician. While the democratic principle enters largely
and vitally, and most properly so, into the organization of
American institutions, the government, when properly conducted, is in reality that of a limited democracy; and as
such, it differs as widely from the vile despotism of pure
or simple democracy, as that of the limited monarchy of
England, from the absolute one of Russia. Nothing has so
perplexed impartial observers of our civil troubles, as the
fact, that while the party of the administration, by the general possession of a slight smattering of knowledge, claims
itself to be a somewhat superior class, yet its conduct
throughout, has been marked by a disregard of honour and
of legal rights, and a countenance of constant rioting and
insubordination. Often changing its name, and at this
moment calling itself the republican party, its characteristics
are identically those of the parties which have dominated
in other destructive eras;—anarchy of thought prevailing
among the members, who are turbulent and uncontrolla-
ble, and in fact, entirely ignorant of the principles of government. The most highly cultivated and considerate persons,

whose just and liberal views are due to sober study and reflection, together with the great mass of honest-minded unpretending people, unperverted by the greed of gain, often illiterate, but by an instinctive unsophistic process of reasoning arriving at correct results, are those who best understand and conform to our governmental system. And how brave, and patient, and enduring they have proved themselves. Called into being, by the unhappy civil troubles, for the war had nearly destroyed old parties, though not their principles, history does not afford the example of a party standing so boldly in opposition to the use of usurped power by the administration of government. Unlike the English, who for ten years without a murmur succumbed to Cromwell, or the voiceless French cowering before Robespiere, in the face of a thoroughly organized reign of terror, and of the most reckless tyranny used for its persecution, it has steadily increased in strength ; and as the advance of time more clearly exposed the revolutionary aims of a dominant minority, it has only assumed a bolder tone and firmer opinion. Yet no turbulence, no disregard of law, has been exhibited. With these characteristics of a true aristocracy, this party, composed of men resolved to maintain their equally valuable democratic principles, has calmly stood in dignified and sublime repose, unmoved amid the tempest of a war upon its rights. Such a party cannot be lightly stirred to action ; it may never be; possibly it may expire under the despotism, for absolute power cannot permit the existence of parties. But should it move, it would be fortunate were it to do so as with one mind and a common purpose, depriving, like the burst of volcanic fire, whatever it touched of its organic character, and using it to feed the purifying flame.

It is a mixed government, this of the United States, and one that worked most satisfactorily until its balance was disturbed, by a dominant party at the North rejecting the aristocratic principle, that of independence of the States, when at once were let loose the same frantic passions which raged in the French Revolution. The exception alluded to in the preceding paragraph, is the radical difference arising from the fact that after the institution of monarchy, the inevitable consequence results that the subjects of the baron gradually lose their character as such, and become, by degrees, subjects of the crown; while in a federation, so long as its members exist, each citizen must of necessity continue to remain associated with a State. Like the barons, the States are original, primitive, and self-existing powers; and confederating together they created the limited federal government which, as it grew in strength and became thoroughly established, assumed supremacy over its creators; a tendency incidental it would seem to federations, and perhaps only to be checked by another confederation somewhat resembling in its nature, that of the barons of England at Runnymede. A further resemblance may be traced. After a feudal federation has been effected, in the creation of a baron, the monarch, as an agent, uses the power that has been delegated to him : and the new baron, if an hereditary peer, can, equally with the others, aid in continuing the limitation of that delegated power which created, not only him, but all others, except those who at the birth of the nation, like the thirteen original States with us, established themselves by the use of the force of their organized power. In this sense, by being made equal with them, he becomes one of the primitive powers. He partakes of their nature. Here it becomes necessary to correct an error into which Mr. Francis Lieber has fallen. He says " The king made the Norman-English nobility. The nobility did not make the king " (On Civil Liberty and Self-Government, i. 64.) The Norman nobility undoubtedly existed long before the Conquest. By the transfer to England the nature of their organized power was not altered; they merely acquired new titles ; as well might it be said that an old society moved into a new building, becomes a new society; and it could, therefore, just as confidently, and more correctly, be stated that, the Norman-English nobility made the king. The king did not make the nobility. And so in the admission of a new State. The act in reality is that of the States, inasmuch as it is the result of their power, but it is performed by their agent, the Federal Government, to whom they expressly delegated the power to 'perform it. This view would remove the perplexity of those who consider the Union to be the parent of the State. It merely appears to be so, because authorized to use a portion of the inherent power of the States to effect precisely that object. A new State is the peer of the other States, and can join them in continuing to limit the delegated central power. An unconstitutional attempt to introduce a new State, as in the instance of Western Virginia, cannot be settled by the senatorial representatives of the States, consenting to receive among them Senators from it; for the States, who are the ultimate judges of the acts of their agent, exist elsewhere than in the Federal Senate. This instance of Western Virginia may be likened to the case of the patent issued in 1856, to Sir James Parke, creating him Baron Wensleydale for life. The peers loudly protested against the intrusion of a life-peer to sit among them, for were all new creations to be such, in time, as hereditary peerages expired, the constitution would be vitally changed, or, perhaps, lost, and therefore, after a full consideration of the subject, he was rejected. "The crown was *forced to submit* to the decision of the Lords; and Lord Wensleydale soon afterwards took his seat, under a new patent, as an hereditary peer of the realm." [May's Constitutional Hist. of England, i. 249.]

It was proposed to insert in the Articles of Constitution an authority for Congress "to call forth the force of the Union against any member of the Union failing to fulfill its duty under the articles thereof." (Elliott's Debates, v. 128.) Mr. Madison said, "A union of States containing such an in-

8

gredient seemed to provide for its own destruction." (Ibid,
140.) Mr. Hamilton considered the idea as so preposterous
that he could say little more than that, "It is impossible."
(Ibid, 200.) The proposition was unanimously rejected.
(Ibid, 140.) While the denial of the power of coercion
would seem to be so clear that it does not admit of argument, for it is simply a question of fact, the prevalence of
the unconstitutional idea, to which Washington referred,
made it essential, that any remaining trace of doubt should
be removed. The struggle, one that unhappily yet continues, first occurred on the question of the adoption of the
Constitution, and as though Providence designed to aid the
blindness of man in this favoured land, a compromise was
effected by the adoption of the ten amendments. Though
not more binding than the body of the instrument, they
are infinitely more emphatic, inasmuch as they were intended to set at rest the points in dispute, upon which
questions had already arisen agitating the country. And
it is remarkable that in the three great convulsions which
have marked its history, the administration of the Federal
Government has not only assumed the power of coercion,
which was unanimously refused by the States, but has invaded the powers or rights reserved to the States or the
people, by one or more of these ten amendments; and
which Washington said were reserved even without them.
No one would would venture to deny this in the matter of
the Alien and Sedition Laws; nor would any one who entirely understood the subject, hold a different view as to the
Force Bill in the time of the Nullification of South Carolina.
With regard to existing affairs, the President now in office,
in a message, has boldly taken the position, that he violated
the Constitution and disregarded his oath, to such an extent
as he thought proper. Prior to these acts of resistance by
some of the States, against the usurpation of power by a
party which happened to administer the central government,
there was a resistance, begun by Massachusetts, in which

all became combined, against the usurpations of the government of England. This continual and successful resistance has not been at the cost of liberty; on the contrary, it has been the means of preserving it. And it should be impressed on every mind, that the four periods of resistance have exactly marked the duration of successive generations of man, as though the memory of freedom did not survive, and each for itself had to struggle for the prize: for the first occurred about the year 1770, the others about the years 1800, 1830, and 1860. From these facts of resistance alone, and altogether independently of the evidence and conclusions previously given, it is seen that the State or Colony, in its revolt, possessed power which it could use, and that it used it successfully; and that after it had entered into the Federal Union, there has not been wanting the full evidence that its power had not ceased to exist. The fact of the power would not seem to be an open question.

We are now further to inquire whether the power has a legal and recognized existence, that is, whether when a State acts altogether independently, the power it wields is its own or is wrested from some other government. It might very well be claimed that the power used by the English subjects in the revolt of the Colonies, legitimately belonged to the Crown, which, however, by its attempted usurpations, forfeited its right thereto, whereupon it became legally vested in the bodies politic formed by the successful rebels. But it has never been held that one State acting against central government, uses the power of another State. The pretence is that in acceding to the Federal Union, it parted with all power; and that when it so acts, it usurps power from it. That is, it is pretended that the Federal Government is an unlimited sovereignty. But this idle and pretentious claim vanishes when we look at the agreements of the States in their Articles of Constitution. The word people is both singular and plural. In the Constitution it is used in the plural number. The preamble of Mr. Pinckney's plan, of the 29th of May, 1787, as did also that reported by Mr. Rutledge, on behalf of the committee, Aug. 6th, commenced, "We the people of New Hampshire, Massachusetts, etc. etc.," each State being named. This preamble was adopted unanimously, but obviously on the suggestion that some of the States might not accede to the Union, the State of Rhode Island not even being present in the Convention, all their names were struck out, and the word " United" inserted by Mr. Morris, who, as Madison says, gave the *finish* to the style and arrangement of the reported draft and subsequent resolutions. (Elliott's Debates, v. 129, 376, 382, and i. 507.) The enacting clause places it beyond even cavil that its Articles were the agreements of States.— " The ratification of the Conventions of nine States shall be sufficient for the establishment of this Constitution *between* the *States* so ratifying the same ;" not *over* the States, nor the people of the States. We may perceive that only a limited and clearly defined power was delegated, for the agreement *between* the *States* is that " the powers *not delegated* to the United States, nor prohibited by it to the States, are reserved to the States *respectively*, or the people." And the preservation of the powers which the States reserved to themselves and their people, is secured and guarded by many recognitions, among others, " the right of the people to be secure in their persons, houses and papers," that of " freedom of speech and of the press ;" and that " a well regulated militia being necessary to the security of a *free State*, the right of the people to keep and bear arms shall not be infringed." There is also the recognition of the separate and distinct organizations of " the militia of the several States." The State then possesses "power;" the Constitution uses that word ; and as its machinery of legislation is perfect, it necessarily can use that power. By the same mode as they act on any other subject, its people, who can only be guided and impelled by their minds, which cannot be coerced, if they conceive it to be a measure necessary for the preservation of their recognized, not granted, nor guaranteed, personal rights, can by their convention and their votes, repeal their ordinance of accession to the Federal Union : and by their arms prepare to maintain their act. In considering such an act, which we cannot deny to be an exercise of power, the real question for us, as it is a violation of a joint compact, is whether it is a *rightful* or *wrongful* exercise of power, for neither the intention of those who bring about the action, nor the result of the action, in the least possible degree affects the nature of the power they use : not more than the nature of the knife or the poison is changed by the difference of intention in its use.

Among sovereigns there is no superior. One does not direct the affairs of another : the moment this occurs, the result is one sovereign power, not two, for one becomes subjugated to the other. Each therefore is equal, each is independent. Its acts are to be taken as the result of its judgment with a view to promote its interest. Does it err, it suffers. A sovereign claims that the use of its power, is the result of its considerate will, and is for its benefit, and that no other can consistently interfere. It therefore holds that its *power* is its *right*, and the two words become almost synonymous. Arrived at this point, only a single step is required to reach, in a degraded monarchy, the doctrine of the Divine right of Kings, or in simple democracy, always fitful when unlimited, the equally false dogma, Vox Populi, Vox Dei. But in governments which have true constitutions, the words in question are employed with more precision than is the case when used by warlike tribes in their conquests, founding nations, or by old or expiring, or apparently expiring nationalities, on which ceaserism threatens to settle, or has already fastened itself. Thus, that English Parliament, which heard the great Earl of Chatham defy the throne when he said, "My Lords! I re-

joice that America has resisted," heard him also say,
"*Power* without *right* is the most detestable object that can
be offered to the human imagination: it is not only perni-
cious to those whom it subjects, but works its own destruction." In the Federal Constitution, except in one
instance, Art. X, of Amendments, which reserves the illim-
itable residue, the word *power* would seem to be used to express that limited amount thereof, which the States have
delegated to the separate departments of the Federal Government which they created : and the word *right*, to express
that which belongs absolutely to each person of the State.
It is in the collected people of the State, the body politic,
that the supreme and absolute sovereignty is recognized as
inherent. In this sense it is scarcely possible in our system,
also, when speaking of a State, which, if separated from
the Union, becomes an unlimited sovereignty, to separate power from right, otherwise than to view it as an
effect resulting from a cause ; for if the people are supreme in their rights, they necessarily are also supreme in
their power. The States delegated none of their people's
rights, they merely delegated a part of that power which is
the result of those rights. Certainly their agents cannot
rightfully transcend the amount of power entrusted to them,
and invade those rights, for that would result in the assumption of supreme power by the agents, who would
thereby become the sovereign power ; and the loss of all
rights by the people, who would consequently sink to the
condition of subjects. To speak with exactness, the word
right means legal moral power. It is so used in the Articles
of Constitution, for instance, in the recognition of the right
to keep arms. This is a right, not conferred or granted
thereby, but recognized as pre-existing and inherent. It
was, as has been stated, acquired by success in arms against
England, and, as is also the case with regard to the other
rights, appears to be recognized as personal, not pertaining
to the State, but to each individual thereof. A State there-

fore, formed as it is of a voluntary association of individuals, though undoubtedly it could assume the power to do so, could not rightfully deprive any one individual of these rights, even if it were unanimous except as to that person. Were it wrongfully to do so, as one man could not successfully maintain his rights against a multitude resolved to be disloyal to their agreement, and to rebel against the principle of their government, of course there would be nothing left for him but enslavement, or else, expatriation or secession, which would remain his right, for the State would not be a voluntary association unless he could withdraw from it. By Section XXV, of the Declaration of Rights of the State of Pennsylvania, the expressed and unquestionable right to do this is recognized.

As each State is a voluntary association of individuals, so the Union is a voluntary association of States, the objects in view being "to establish justice, insure domestic tranquility, provide for the common defence, promote the general welfare, and secure the blessings of liberty to ourselves and our posterity." And more completely to secure these distinctly stated objects, the States agreed that alterations of the articles could be made by three fourths of them agreeing thereto. This preserves the principle of consent, but it involves another principle, that no alteration be made touching the independence of a State, or the right of any person. Now the States which might agree to an alteration, could do so were the majority in each to be but one vote, and they might all be the lesser States; whereas the vote in the States opposing the alteration could be unanimous, and these might all be the greater States. Thus, as by the census of 1860, the eight greater States contain a population of 16,197,127, while the twenty-six lesser States contain 14,950,698. Now to one half of this latter number add one for each of the twenty-six States, and we have 7,475,375, very considerably less than one-fourth of the population, who could legally make an alteration against the will of 23,673,476, the entire population of the eight greater States and one half (lacking one for each) of that of the twenty-six lesser States. This is on the basis of an election for members of the Convention by a general ticket throughout a State. If each district in a State should elect a member, the minority could be very much further reduced. This conclusively proves that the people of all the States do not form one body politic, for in such a society the rule of the majority prevails. Were an alteration so made, to be of a nature similar to some of the acts of the present Executive, to the effect, for example, that the people should not have the right to keep arms, could folly itself suppose that so great a violation of the principles on which the federal compact was founded would be permitted? So far as form and words were concerned, it would clearly be the law, no lawyer and no judge could gainsay that. No pamphleteers would be required to furnish, as in other cases of violation of the Constitution, an interminable amount of chop-logic, unanswerable because unintelligible, to prove what every one could see. They would be dumb, for the letter of the law would speak for itself. Yet would not the people be silent. They would show that a power existed in the land beyond the letter of the law. The spirit of liberty would manifest itself, and renew the spirit of the law.

Let us suppose another case. No State can, without its own consent, be deprived of its equal representation in the Senate. Were, however, the 31,036,609 people of thirty-three of the States to unanimously resolve that as the State of Delaware had but 112,216, it should therefore have but one Senator, and alter the agreement to that effect, it would be submitted to; because sufficient power did not exist to prevent it. It may however be well supposed that this easy, quiet and successful usurpation of power in a case apparently trivial, would be fraught with more danger and result in a greater revolution, than would the other case; for once excited, the lust of power is insatiable; and unrestrained,

it would sweep on until it leveled every barrier in the dust.
Whereas, in the case previously supposed, power would
merely be used for the maintenance of the barriers of resistance, and with success, its use would most probably
terminate.

From the view that has been presented, it is to be supposed
that in the withdrawal of a State from the Union, the end
sought is conservation of that State, certainly not the destruction of another, much less of itself; nor is the government of the Federal Union among the remaining States
necessarily less perfect, except in the degree resulting from
the degradation of the principle of union, owing to the increased power of domination in a party animated by the
fell spirit of unconstitutional aims. Nor does a State withdraw because of its objection to the pre-existing and yet
existing terms of Union. But it is because of a declaration
by a majority of the States that *they* will no longer consider
themselves bound by those agreements, and that the minority must submit to have imposed upon them,—not new
terms of agreement, for consent is necessary to agreement,
but terms to which they will *not* agree. It is because the
principle of *consent*, the sole foundation of the whole system
of free and federal government, is about to be abandoned,
and no longer recognized: and as a consequence, that
another principle, *force*, a principle upon which each State
itself is based, but one altogether repugnant to the federal
system, is to reign undisputed through the future. Owing
to the frequency of elections, the interests and social
conditions existing in a State, and the opinions which prevail, are at all times faithfully and exactly represented in
its internal government. The people of a State can therefore by no possibility desire revolution, other than that
which is always going on with them. It is impossible, for
at their will they make such change as they desire. Their
abandoning the manifold advantages which are so well
known to result from union, would therefore seem to make
9

it conclusive, so far as the people of the withdrawing State were concerned, that their act was solely with a view to prevent a revolution, which was going on in other States, from reaching them. It cannot be supposed that a single State, or any number of them, being a minority, but acting singly, as they necessarily must at first, would attempt to dominate the majority. But it can be supposed that a majority of the States acting, as a political party, through the machinery of the Federal Government, might attempt to dominate the minority; and the intention in their attempt would be, and could only be, to effect a revolution against the will of, and in, the minority States. In the event then of the withdrawal of a State, wisdom and knowledge would lead our minds to the belief, that sober reflection may with time bring a conviction, that the extreme act was a rightful exercise of its power; or it may prove otherwise; for it is time alone which dispels the clouds of ignorance as well as of passion, and finds, on one side or the other, a modified opinion, and in both, a kindly temper favourable to a compromise.

It may then be considered as settled, that a State in withdrawing from the Union uses its power. This cannot be controverted. The fact is so, and the law is so. The fact that it has done so may be disagreeable to us—it is more sadly so than can be comprehended by those who do not understand the nature of the government,—and we may have no knowledge of the law; yet must we be careful lest *we* transgress; for ignorance of the law excuseth no man. But a State's rightful or wrongful use of that power is another and an open question, and one upon which each man has a right to form his own deliberate opinion; he has, however, no moral right to the indulgence of incendiary utterances, whose only meaning is the destruction of established power. If the act be recognized, and the State considered as a foreign government, then the Federal Government may rightfully hold it to account for violating the compact into which it had entered, because the States delegated to the Federal Government the power to make war upon foreign governments. But war cannot be rightfully and constitutionally made upon a State by the Federal Government, so long as it claims that State as belonging thereto, because the States, as has been shown, expressly, and the vote was unanimous, withheld the power to use force against a State belonging to the Union. Force was authorized to be used only against persons. If used against States it is wrongful, it is usurped power, and violates the compact with States yet belonging to the federation, and the rights of persons in them, and would, if successful result in the destruction of the States, and the loss of rights on the part of the citizens. It therefore increases the numbers of those opposed to abandoning the constitutional principles of the government, and must, if persisted in, ultimately result in the withdrawal of yet other States. It would be attempted, but vainly attempted, to prevent this, by the suppression of all power in those States whose votes exhibited a change of opinion,–vainly, because State organization, once suppressed, there would arise in its place an armed party organization, for which the people and the States have provided by their Bills of Rights, and to maintain which the physical ability exists. And that armed party would be of the majority, for the conclusive reason, that so long as a party continued in a minority its suffrage would not be violated, and it could not, as a matter of course, be brought to arm. But were the Administration of the Federal Government to succeed in retaining the consent of the people of the States now supporting it, to the use of power, which it is admitted by all, is extra-constitutional, the whole nature, form, and character, and eventually the name, of the Northern Government must become changed; one consolidated State replacing the union of many. The Southern States, on the other hand, if successful in maintaining their independence, will continue to have a government of States united, scarcely differ-

jecting. In providing for the rendition of fugitives from
service, there was to guide them and us, the Epistle of St.
Paul returning Onesimus.

No one who has written on the subject, has been more
unqualified in his assent to the principle of secession, than
John Quincy Adams. He speaks of it as a right vested in
the people of every State. "Thus stands the RIGHT," he
says, and by printing the word in capitals, instead of italics,
he more than emphasises it. Mr. Adams says "It is not
immaterial to remark that the signers of the Declaration,
though qualifying themselves as the Representatives of the
United States of America in general Congress assembled,
yet issue the Declaration in the name and by the authority
of the good people of the colonies, and that they declare,
not each of the separate colonies, but the *united colonies* free
and independent States." (Oration by J. Q. Adams, 50th
Anniversary N. Y. His. Soc., 1839, p. 15.) "There was no
congeniality of principle between the Declaration of Independence and the Articles of Confederation." (Ibid, 17.)
"The right of a single State or of several States in combination together to secede from the Union, has been directly
asserted, frequently controverted, etc., * * * * but is
now terminating in a more devoted adherence and willing
subserviency to the authority of the Union. * * * *
With these qualifications, we may admit the same right as
vested in the *people* of every State in the Union, with reference to the general government, which was exercised by
the people of the United Colonies, with reference to the
supreme head of the British Empire, of which they formed
a part—and under these limitations, have the people of each
State in the Union a right to secede from the Confederated
Union itself. Thus stands the RIGHT." (Ibid, 67, 68, 69.)

It is not too much to say that there is not the slightest
trace of an idea that the people of all the Colonies or States,
ever formed themselves into one body politic. Every atom
of evidence is directly to the contrary. What was proposed

by New Hampshire (see ante p. 14) would have effected that result; but her proposal was not even made a subject of discussion. Up to July 1776, the Colonies were making constitutions, which, in view of the continued sovereignty of the Crown, they styled temporary. Virginia, however, formed for herself a constitution without any such provision ; but in order to make the act a logical one, she had, on the 29th of June, 1776, declared the government "as formerly exercised by the Crown of Great Britain, totally dissolved." (Elliot's Debates, i. 66.) The Declaration of Independence was proposed, in Congress, by the Delegates from Virginia, under instructions from that State to propose, not only that measure, but also "a Confederation to bind the Colonies more closely together." (Ibid, i, 56.) As it was five years before this proposed Confederation was at last agreed to by every State, one after another, it is utterly incomprehensible that they could by their Declaration, as Judge Story holds, have ceased to be States : [Ibid, i. 66.] and this without any one suspecting it. That in the assertion of independence they assumed to be States, and afterwards continued in the same condition, cannot be controverted, because, on all questions, in both the Continental Congress and in that of the Confederation, all votes were by States; as it now is in the event of a failure of the Electoral College to elect a President. On the first of July, 1776, on the motion to adopt the Declaration, the two members from Delaware were divided: the following day, however, the scale was turned by the appearance of a third member. [Ibid, 59, 60.] The action of this State, through its embassy, was unquestionably that of a political unit. And such was also the case with that of each of the States. A vague idea of the exact nature of the result that followed from the position assumed by the Colonies, has no doubt arisen from the use, and it was a proper use, in the Declaration of Independence, of the word *unanimous*. It merely conveys the idea of a fact, and it means nothing beyond that, unless, indeed, in connection with the absence of the names of the Colonies, the hope was entertained that Canada would in time be included in the revolt. Had this occurred, the absence of her name, if those of the others had appeared, would probably have proved an obstacle in future negotiations. Had Gen. Montgomery captured Quebec, under the term *United Colonies*, undoubtedly the Province of Canada would have been claimed. In the revolutionary period there were two principal questions, and only two; and in these unanimity was essential. The first was resistance against the tyranny of England; and out of this grew the second, which was the dissolution of the dependence on its Crown. Had any colony determined on non-resistance, or on a continuance of British sovereignty, certainly the others could not have undertaken to effect for it, what it would, in that event, have been opposed to; which was actually the case with the Province of Canada. On the minor questions, those which regarded the measures by which the two principal ones could most effectually be established, unanimity was not required.

As to the assertion that " there was no congeniality of principle between the Declaration of Independence and the Articles of Confederation," nothing more need be said than that, as they were both proposed by the same men, in the same instructions, to the same men, and both were adopted by the same States, it is fair to presume and claim, that the people of that day believed it a question of not the slightest importance whether they were, or were not congenial; and if such was their belief, it need require no violent effort to be also ours.

Without commenting on his use of the word *subserviency*, which has no place in the vocabulary of freemen, it may be remarked, that Mr. Adams' admission of the principle of secession as a right vested in the people of a State, seems too broad and sweeping in its character. Their vested power is exclusive, but in view of the compact of the States,

while they have a right of judgment as to the propriety of
its exercise, it is not an exclusive right. He probably had
in his mind the ordinary case, wherein the only organized
power is that of the one national government, without a
true constitution, and consequently unprovided with a mode
of changing rulers, where undoubtedly, as it is the only
possible means, the clear and unqualified right, if the word
be used as the synonym of power, of revolution exists.
But federations differ from simple national governments.
He had not, perhaps, considered that in our system, the
people of a State live under two governments; their own,
always appointed by themselves, and directed by their
will; and the federal, appointed, as to its administration,
perhaps, exclusively by other States, and directed, perhaps,
by the will of hostile majorities living exclusively in those
other States. And that therefore, so far as the seceding
State is concerned, the rupture of the federal relation need
not necessarily be, except as to one of its governments, of
a revolutionary, and much less of an anarchial, character.
It has previously been shown that the withdrawal of a State
would be because of the revolutionary tendency of other
States ; a tendency boding all the ills of social war, not at
first amongst themselves, but directed against the State,
that, with a view to check that tendency extending to itself, would engage in a measure which, however essential
for the preservation of its existence, would certainly be at
the hazard of a conflict of arms ; but by which, however,
it would escape the greater horrors of anarchy and dire
social war. Generally among men a successful revolution
is pronounced to be right; for an existing sovereignty
could scarcely admit that its title to power was to be traced
to a wrong. But there is a higher view by which to judge
of human affairs than by this vulgar mode of measurement.
By considering the corrrectness of the principles involved,
and the elevated aims of the unfortunate, we may often
justly hold that those who fail have been in the right ; and,

on the other hand, that those who succeed, however remarkable their energy or respectable their ability, may nevertheless have been grievously in the wrong. It is thus we
judge the people of other lands. Mr. Adams has passed
away, leaving his well considered opinion that if separation
should come, it ought to be in peace. He would have
held that American to be a reckless man, who, claiming that
we alone have adopted the maxim, that "government
derives its just powers from the consent of the governed;"
and that we alone can, by the ballot, ascertain consent; yet
vaunts before the world his delight at usurped power crush-
ing consent; and at force and corruption violating and pol-
luting the ballot by which alone it is possible to ascertain it.

It has been attempted to show that the constitutional
power of the Federal Government is, as it was intended it
should be, strictly limited, like that of the Crown of England; and by the same made—*the only possible one*—the
withholding from it the supreme and absolute power of
command over the arms and armed men of the country:
that this is the direct result of the principle of federation,
appearing wherever that principle can be traced; and that
when the best men of the land lose the disposition to be their
own defenders that principle disappears. And it may not
be doubted that so long as this constitutional limitation of
power is recognized; so long as it is held to be the supreme
law that a State possesses power that it can use at will; so
long as it is believed that one State has no right to interfere in the affairs of another, just so long will our free institutions endure. .But when sophists delude them, men's
enervated minds become, as it were, saturated with the un-
wholesome fogs of the muddy and stagnant swamps of
lifeless twaddle, instead of filled with bounding vigour in-
spired by healthful draughts of the knowledge of principles,
sought at their clear and lucid fountain heads. And they
call it *progress* as they are lured on through dark and tangled
wastes by some short-lived jack o' the lantern, bred of the
pestilential vapours which surround them. And that a

master may think, and act, and be responsible for them, and save them, as they vainly hope, from the sloughs from which they have lost the ability to escape, they agree that power shall no longer remain divided, and listlessly consent to drop the arms from hands once nerved by the spirit of liberty. Thus they yield themselves, their bodies and their minds, to the keeping of a despot, for whatever may be his intention or his character, the possessor of undivided power must, by the law of its nature, draw the rivets from every association within its sphere, like the loadstone island, which, as the ship of Sinbad the Sailor approached, drew from it the spikes which held its planks together, tumbling them an useless wreck upon its shore.

Liberty and progress co-exist with, and are fostered by, the division of power, while anarchy, which ever attends a war of principles, and these are potent and conflicting in this Northern land, must, perhaps for very many years, reign the undisputed monarch through the fearful, yet, ultimately, unsuccessful struggle for its consolidation. The only escape from this dreaded fate is through a return to the true principle of the federal system ; for the real and actual division of power in this country, is the very soul and spirit of all its institutions ; it pervades all the foundations, and it appears in all the superstructures. Each State is based upon it, for by the sword it wrested it from England, and it was intended that its organization, as well as that of the Federal Government, should wield it. Contiguity does not affect it, for adjoining States may, as they choose to will, use opposing power, while widely separated ones may will to use it in a similar direction. Every citizen is bound by this division of power, for it is the law and the Constitution. He that is opposed to it is the really disloyal, if that word applies in our system, for, as a member of a body politic, he has plighted his faith to support it. Yet while he is bound by it, and it is his duty to submit to it, he has the right, if he think proper to do so, to propose and urge its alteration ; but he has the right to do so, only in the mode the Law and Constitution point out. Does he, when entrusted with administration, venture to assume and use power which has not been delegated to the Federal Government, or he who urges him so entrusted, to assume and use such power, he becomes lawless ; his object is revolution ; he strikes at the Constitution ; he would destroy it. He it is that aims at the national life. He is the architect of ruin ; and his crime is more heinous than that of the regicide, for he seeks to destroy a constellation of sovereigns.

An accurate, and it is thought to be a moderate estimate of the debt of the Federal Government, liquidated and unliquidated, is, that it already amounts, and without any indication of a termination to its increase, to full four thousand millions of dollars. While in principal equal to, the interest on it will be double, that of Great Britain. The valuation of British property is, however, three times that of the Northern States, so that the burden on Americans, and soon it will begin to be felt, is actually six times that on Englishmen. There is no ordinary peril in this. The organized institutions of the country may, possibly, even yet be restored, and with them a constitutional government somewhat resembling that of England in its nature and its success; but it will be found to be an impossibility to continue more than a few years longer the present enforced unity of government, whose fall must necessarily involve along with its own, that of the most overstrained financial system that has yet been presented to the world. Montesquieu ascribes the facility with which the Mahometans made their conquests, to the overtaxation of the Empire ; it having reached such a point that "Anastasius invented a tax for breathing." (The Spirit of Laws, i. 310.) Their conquests could not have been effected at all, much less with such facility, had the people of the Empire been their own soldiers. But their day for that was over; had they, however, been so, they themselves would have prevented, or if not, they would have cured, the disorder of over taxation. The melancholy truth seems to be, that the old

age of national life brings with it, an administration of
government controlled by, or in the hands of, the extrava-
gant moneyed class, who, with adverse interests, always
distrust the people; a standing army of foreign mercena-
aries, an establishment so unstable, that, when it has exhausted the country which requires for its defence arms
more valiant than its own, it either possesses itself of that
country, or else quickly disappears, like water in sand: a
disuse of arms among the people who, by that time, have
abandoned the simple mode of life of their hardy and self-
reliant forefathers; and a taxation so onerous as to amount to
positive spoliation. When plunged in such condition, a nation
has passed its era of making conquests. This shirt of Nessus
has been slipped upon the American people by men whose
rapturous applause, at their own success, drowned the soft
and gentle footfalls of the avenging gods, who, in their ap-
proaches. as heathen story tells, are ever shod with wool.
Yet there were not wanting those who gave utterance to
their alarm; but they were unheeded, and often silenced by
the cry that they were disloyal, and not patriotic ; the low
voice of innocence was stifled by loud-mouthed crime. Patriotism! And what is it? As to its possession, the same re-
ply may be given that the venerable and Reverend Dr. Alex-
ander made to the conceited student of divinity, who enquired
of him "Whether he had any religion?" "None to *speak* of.
young man!" And so with patriotism or loyalty. The man
who speaks of it is not to be trusted, for he is without it as
surely as the man who vaunts his honour is without that
quality: or as the woman who could condescend to dicuss
the question of her virtue, must not only possess it not, but
must also, be without a comprehension of what it is. Men
may differ widely, they may be in grievous error, and yet
possess patriotism. He who, by mad fanaticism, ruins his
country, is not, necessarily, without it. It is a quality
possessed by every one who boasts not of it, who trades not
in it: and truly did Dr. Johnson say of those who do, that
"Patriotism is the last refuge of a scoundrel."